AF405769

THE *Untapped*
TEAM
ADVANTAGE

Building Team Connections
as a Leadership Choice

PRAISE FOR
THE UNTAPPED TEAM ADVANTAGE

The Untapped Team Advantage is compassionate and wise. Author Cauwelier reminds readers that building a team is not like building a house because the work of building a team is never done. It's more like joining a gym; if you resolve to get fit, you understand it means resolving to stay fit. Teams require continual nurturing and pivoting—and cannot be led with a simple checklist approach. The book's compelling stories and practical advice shine the spotlight on the relationships among a team's members as the source of greater engagement and performance.

– Amy C. Edmondson
  Professor, Harvard Business School
  Author, *The Fearless Organization: Creating Psychological Safety in the Workplace for Learning, Innovation, and Growth (Wiley 2019)*

A clear and comprehensive guide to leading teams. Dr. Peter Cauwelier touches on almost every subject a team leader needs to know—what skills are necessary, how you develop them, how you build teams, what you do when conflict erupts and so on. This book is an excellent guide to team-building for someone newly assigned to a team. It also offers important advice for executives of companies that are considering a team approach to management.

—   Philippe Bonnet
    Global Vice President Human Resources, Essilor
    Singapore

Having had the opportunity to participate in the transition to high-performing teams in my previous company, Peter Cauwelier has captured and simplified the journey in this book. His roadmap removes all the "noise" associated with years of team-based learnings to focus on the key principles and tools necessary to drive engagement, collaboration, and focus. I wish I had this book years ago.

—   Clare Amrhein
    Market HR Manager, Walmart
    USA

A very realistic description of team dynamics, and a pragmatic and highly practical guide to develop and sustain successful teams. *The Untapped Team Advantage* will truly speak to all operational managers!

– Fredrik Schyberg
  Senior Vice President Operations, Essilor
  Thailand

Leaders win games, teams win championships... Peter's inspiring book will definitely help you look at your team differently, and redefine your role and responsibility as a team leader. Keep on growing your teams and help them realize their full potential!

– Jean-Francois Couve
  General Manager, GSK Consumer Healthcare
  Thailand

It can't get any more practical than this. If you are in the business of leading or building teams, get a copy and acquire the wisdom contained in this book!

– Mark Relova
  Vice President and Head, Troo Lab
  Philippines

If you aren't already convinced about the power of a high-performance team, read this book. With an engaging and clear writing style and rich leadership background, Peter offers compelling evidence that a leader with the right mindset and approach can significantly enhance a team's performance.

— Shannon Banks
  Director, Be Leadership
  United Kingdom

This book is a straightforward read that clears up some hardcore misconceptions about the power of teams. It makes us see teams for what they truly are, valuable assets with limitations. The book is filled with practical tips that are easy to apply and founded on research and solid concepts.

— Mies de Koning
  Action Learning New York
  USA

Great teams are built on continuous co-learning. This engaging book provides practical advice on how to create the conditions for co-learning that leads to high performance.

—   Professor David Clutterbuck
    Practice Lead at Coaching and Mentoring International
    United Kingdom

THE *Untapped* TEAM ADVANTAGE

Building Team Connections as a Leadership Choice

PETER CAUWELIER

Candid Creation Publishing

First published 2020

Copyright © 2020 Peter Cauwelier

All rights reserved. No part of this publication may be reproduced, stored in a retrieval system, or transmitted, in any form or by any means, electronic, mechanical, photocopying, recording or otherwise, without the prior permission of the publisher, except for inclusion of brief quotations in a review.

Candid Creation Publishing books are available through most major bookstores in Singapore. For bulk order of our books at special quantity discounts, please email us at enquiry@candidcreation.com.

THE UNTAPPED TEAM ADVANTAGE

Author   : Peter Cauwelier
Publisher   : Phoon Kok Hwa
Editor   : Tansey Tang
Cover designer   : Ryanne Ng
Layout   : Corrine Teng
Published by   : Candid Creation Publishing LLP
                   167 Jalan Bukit Merah
                   #05-12 Connection One Tower 4
                   Singapore 150167
Website   : www.candidcreation.com
Facebook   : www.facebook.com/CandidCreationPublishing
Email   : enquiry@candidcreation.com

National Library Board, Singapore Cataloguing-in-Publication Data

Names: Cauwelier, Peter.
Title: The untapped team advantage : building team connections as a leadership choice / Peter Cauwelier.
Description: Singapore : Candid Creation Publishing, 2020.
Identifiers: OCN 1193183794 | ISBN 978-981-14-7366-1 (paperback)
Subjects: Teams in the workplace--Management. | Teams in the workplace--Training of. | Leadership.
Classification: DDC 658.4022--dc23

CONTENTS

PREFACE

I have seen many teams in my career. I have been a member of many and I have had the opportunity to lead a number of teams. In some, all the members were sitting in the same office, and in others, they were geographically spread; some teams comprised members of the same generation and national culture, and others were a mix of generations and cultures; some were dealing with very standardized, routine operations, and others were in the research, development, and engineering sphere. In addition, these teams had different histories, were from companies with different activities, and from varied business environments. It is intriguing that on some teams, it seems that people really enjoy working together, are supported by a great team leader, and achieve their targets and objectives. Then there are teams where team members avoid one another, where work gets done by sending each other messages, and where everybody points to someone else (mostly behind their back) when something goes wrong. When I ask those in dysfunctional teams what they had tried to do to work better together, or what they were planning to do to improve the situation, it was clear they had given up on one another and on the team. They were all aware the situation was pretty bad, but didn't really know how to move into a better place.

To further explore how teams interact and develop, I completed my doctoral thesis on the topic of team learning, in particular how the connections between team members impact the way a team learns, and how this learning in turn develops the knowledge in the team, either about the topic the team is dealing with or about the team and its members. My research experiment compared several teams going through the same team challenge and I saw again how different the interactions were from one team to the next, and how this impacted the way each team completed the challenge. These teams were made up of equally capable professionals, yet some teams just went around in circles without making any progress while others built upon each team member's questions and ideas to move towards resolving the challenge.

In my professional experience and doctoral research, I didn't come across or identify a magic formula to develop teams. And I am quite sure there is none. At the same time, I want you to know that you can improve your team's connections and therefore its performance, probably by a lot.

This book is written for leaders who have a team, and for members who belong to a team. It is for those who believe that teams are the core of improved performance and that more can be achieved from developing teams— or those who will believe that after reading Part One. It is for those who believe that it is their own responsibility to get the best out of the people who are on their team. And finally, it is for those who are already convinced of the importance of teams, but have been struggling to find concrete ways to get more out of their team.

My goal with this book is three-fold, with each objective representing one Part.

In Part One, I invite you to think about teams—for real: think about your own responsibility when it comes to developing a team, think about the untapped possibilities teams represent, and also acknowledge that very often the realities surrounding you do not favor teams as a leadership choice. In the end, it is your choice to develop your leadership through teams, or not.

If by the end of Part One you are convinced that teams really represent an extraordinary untapped advantage, you will keep on reading, and in Part Two, I present approaches, models, and techniques for building and developing a team. I also make clear that certain steps are useless if the preceding ones have been skipped, or worse, implemented and then abandoned. The basic steps do not represent a menu from which to select a few, but are really the minimum requirements. In the section on growing the team, I invite you to explore the next phase once the basics are in place, focusing on developing a level of psychological safety in the team that is the foundation of sustained performance.

Then in Part Three, there are no more techniques or tips but rather new ideas to inspire you once again that so much more is possible when it comes to getting the best out of people through teams. Although the team is your limit, this part shows that there really is no limit to how a team can develop. It also invites you to think about the kind of leader you want to be, and what kind of memories you want to form for those you work with.

In Parts Two and Three we also introduce James and Susan in a tale of two teams. James and Susan are fictional characters based on leaders with whom I have worked. Both start a new responsibility as team leader in a new job and face certain challenges to which they react differently, either deliberately or unconsciously. Certainly, their paths diverge quickly, and 18 months into their new jobs, they are in very different situations and states of mind. The tale of two teams illustrates that building a team is not a box to tick off but rather a leadership choice. Building a team— or not—happens through the daily actions, decisions, and communications made. Although James and Susan are team leaders, their tales will also resonate with those who are members of a team.

Thank you to all the teams I have had the chance to work with and support, both in a professional setting as well as in my doctoral research. It is through them and their stories that I have developed the content of this book. And I hope that sharing these experiences will be beneficial to many more teams.

INTRODUCTION

ased on Michael Watkins' international bestseller *The First 90 Days*, authors, consultants, and gurus tell you that in the first 90 days in a new job, you need to hit a few key objectives to set you up for near-guaranteed success. One of these is to "clean shop", getting rid of those who don't belong on the team and showing that contrary to your (most likely unsuccessful) predecessor, you mean business. You will send the clear message to those who are allowed to stay—and more importantly, those that hired you!—that you are tough, and everyone had better get aligned. Getting rid of the weak or bad apples is a necessary step if you want to succeed. As the new leader, you show that you are able to make the difficult decisions your predecessor was unable or unwilling to make. With you in the leadership position, things will now—finally!—change.

In his book *From Good to Great*, Jim Collins lists "First Who, Then What" as one of the key requirements to build great organizations:

> Those who build great organizations make sure they have the right people on the bus and the right people in the key seats before they figure out where

to drive the bus. They always think first about who and then about what. When facing chaos and uncertainty, and you cannot possibly predict what's coming around the corner, your best "strategy" is to have a busload of people who can adapt to and perform brilliantly no matter what comes next. Great vision without great people is irrelevant.

Thus, in the first 90 days, the leader will sit down with each of the members of the team to identify the A-players and high-potentials on the one hand, and the losers and misfits on the other. The leader will often decide to get rid of those members of the team with whom he or she feels little or no connection, those who are so different that merely interacting with them brings headaches. For some leaders, it may be the nay-sayers, who question or challenge all the time, or who always come up with a reason why a new idea won't work. Other leaders cannot see the need to keep team members who are stuck in their routine, just getting their job done and never coming up with any breakthrough innovative ideas. Or it may be those who seem to endlessly compromise and hesitate instead of making the hard but necessary decisions. Nearly always, the "wrong" people are those that are very different—in their behaviors, thoughts or manners—from the new leader.

Those that get kicked off the bus get replaced by the "right" people, who are either found internally or are new recruits. In either case, it is the leader who makes the call, and without exception, those who are invited to get on the bus will be people with whom the leader has a great connection. Most often, it will be those who are very much like the leader. The losers are kicked off the bus and the A-players and stars are invited to get on.

After 90 days or so, the new leader has acted on all the initial priorities, and with all the right people now on the bus, is ready to accelerate towards a bright and successful future. What happens after the initial 90 days? Is the bus powerfully driving on to ever-greater adventures, with the driver firmly in control, avoiding any obstacles along the way? Are all the team members now solidly in their assigned seats, enthusiastically putting into action the bus driver's brilliant strategies? Not much is written about year one or year two.

In my experience, things don't look quite as rosy as we would be led to believe. Although the bus driver was off to a flying start, it seems some important bumps are appearing on the road. The new marketing guru who got on the bus, poached from a competitor and seemingly the perfect fit for the job, can't get his team to perform. Half of his team has resigned and there is a constant lack of resources to execute the myriad innovative ideas the marketing manager comes up with. The operations director who was let go, because after more than ten years in the same role she was just too averse to any form of change, is now sorely missed because she at least got the products out on time and on budget. One year after her departure the operations department is in a constant fire-fighting mode, running from one crisis to the next and missing deadlines, which leads to unhappy customers. The new human resources manager was at first a source of inspiration with his toughness and decisiveness after a weak predecessor. But only one year into the job, he faces rejection by most of the people he interacts with and is retreating in his office. Only 18 months after a great start, the new leader seems a bit lost as he tries to juggle all these unexpected challenges. He takes direct control of the biggest crises and has lost confidence in some whom he thought were the "right" people for the bus.

> 66 Whoever is on the bus belongs there! 99
> – Peter Cauwelier

I wholeheartedly disagree with this view of leading a team or an organization. Whoever is on the bus belongs there. It is not about the who first and the what later. It is about the how. Developing a team means strengthening the connections between those who are on the bus. If you view leadership as you confidently driving the bus with your team nicely seated in the back, don't be surprised if people get off when the bus slows down or if the road gets bumpy. The image of the heroic leader taking the loyal followers on an adventurous trip may be inspiring for movies, but it is vastly disconnected from the reality that businesses and organizations are facing. Leadership is about building real teams and delivering performance through these teams.

PART ONE

THINKING ABOUT
Teams

I am biased and I think that teams are the best things around after coffee. But that is me. Maybe you don't think like that, or maybe you're just not convinced yet. Or maybe you haven't really thought that much about teams. In this first part of the book, I invite you to reflect on your own thinking around teams, and to develop it further. Focusing on high-performance teams is your choice as a leader or a team member, and only you can make that choice. Although the potential of teams is great and largely unexploited, there is no simple formula or step-by-step plan to turn that potential into sustained performance. Finally, you are not living in a vacuum and the different realities and contexts in which you function are not always conducive to team development. We will list these different realities as a way to acknowledge the current state of your team and also to highlight the needed changes. Part One of this book raises many questions and has very few answers.

Maybe by the time you reach the end of Part One, you will conclude that you don't really see the potential of a high-performance team, that this team thing is not for you, or that you just have too many things to do. If that is the case, there is no point in reading Parts Two and Three, and even less in trying to implement piecemeal some of the elements described in the rest of the book. If you are not convinced that building teams makes sense, halfheartedly trying out a few interesting new ideas is not meaningful for you or those involved.

Instead, I hope that this first part of the book will inspire you and convince you that the potential benefits that teams bring—for you, for those in the team, and for the organization—are definitely worth focusing your energy on. Then, Parts Two and Three will later give you concrete elements about the basics of building (or re-building) a team and on growing it into a sustainable high-performance team.

IS THIS FOR YOU?

Building a high-performance team
is a leadership choice

A MINDSET, NOT AN ITEM ON THE TO-DO LIST

When you build a house, at some point, you will be done. You may continue to change a few things occasionally, but overall, the house will pretty much remain the way you completed it. Developing a team is not like that. A team is never "done". A leader shared with me that one of the difficulties of building a team was the need to rebuild a team on an average of every two years, because of people leaving and others joining, or because of changes in the organization. That is correct, and it is the inherent nature of developing a team.

Developing a team is more like building up your physical strength by going to the gym. You won't see much change after one week, but you persist because you are committed. There are periods where you go to the gym very often and others where you go more rarely, but your physical fitness journey is definitely not something you do for a certain period, then stop because you consider it done. You are either working on your physical strength or you are not. Developing a high-performance team is like building up your physical strength. It is a habit or a mindset more than an item on the to-do list. The environment in which you are trying to build your team will sometimes make things difficult. There will be change, and you will be faced with people resisting that change. Some of the team members will be below par while others whom you really value may leave the team. Team members from one culture will think and work very differently from those from other cultures. People on your team will be part of other teams, including virtual and remote teams.

In many organizations, the excitement of resolving a crisis is much stronger than the satisfaction of building something where the impact or result will only be visible in the long term. The immediate and short-term priorities seem to take up all our focus and energy every day, and the less urgent objectives like people or team development are put off until things are settled down somewhat. Not taking care of these elements then leads to crises, like when a key team member leaves or when an important project does not deliver because of team misalignment or lack of communication.

Similar to sticking to your physical strength program, there will be many distractions and potential excuses that can keep you from your team development commitment. There will be some setbacks. But I sincerely believe that each team can be improved and that if you maintain a mindset of developing teams as your leadership choice, you will build satisfaction and engagement in those around you, and maybe more importantly, in yourself.

ONLY YOU CAN BUILD YOUR TEAM

Teams are often underappreciated in an organization. There are two sides to this reality. On the one hand, building a high-performance team will most likely not be part of your job description or assigned priorities. You will definitely not get fired for not developing a high-performance team! Building a high-performance team is your personal leadership choice. You need a genuine conviction that building a team is what being a leader is about. You will need strength to persist and resist the frequent temptations to prioritize the other pressures you face each day. At the same time, this situation has the advantage that you nearly always will have a free hand when it comes to building a team. You do not need the approval of the headquarters or the legal department! Building your leadership around teams is a continuously evolving way of working with and developing the people around you. It is a choice that can impact yourself and those in the team around you profoundly.

Getting away with a team once in a while is a great idea, and you can ask experts or your human resources department for support in organizing specific events or team retreats. But that contributes very little to what the team develops into. A team develops through daily routines, interactions, and discussions. There is not a single moment when you do not impact your team, through what you do or say, or what you don't do and don't say. It is really only you who can build your team. It is your choice to take this on or not.

THE TYPE OF TEAMS THIS BOOK IS NOT ABOUT

When you read articles or books about high-performance teams, you often find uplifting stories about US SEAL teams, Mount Everest expedition teams, or teams that went through a near-death, catastrophic experience. The Chilean mine rescue and Thai cave rescue are widely referenced as inspiring examples of teamwork and have been turned into movies. I once received an invitation for a talk about "team lessons from the Yakuza" (I didn't attend)!

These stories are often fascinating and—to an extent—inspirational, but what do you do once you finish reading the article or book or watching the movie? Do you jump into action, implementing what you read or saw? Inspiration is defined as "the process of being mentally stimulated to do or feel something, especially to do something creative." Too often, the inspiration we feel momentarily leads to very few concrete actions. Most likely, you will put the article or book away thinking, "Well, that was interesting… but my situation is so different." Or "Well, these ideas wouldn't work for us for sure!" When we take as a reference or target the 0.01% of teams that do extraordinary things in extraordinary circumstances, we create a huge gap with the reality in which most of us live and work. Instead of finding inspiration that ignites the spark of change and leads to action, these examples are so far removed from our reality that emulating them becomes but a dream.

NO TEN-STEP CHECKLIST

Although I give many examples, tips, and concrete techniques that you can apply to your team, you will not find "10 steps to a high-performance team" in this book. This type of structure may be attractive and easily absorbed, but I simply do not believe that there are 10 steps (or 4 or 15) to build a high-performance team. A framework like this gives the impression that building a team is a task or an almost mechanical activity with a start and end point. Building a team is a mindset and there is no end to it. Just as there is no end to learning or to developing oneself, there is no end to building a team.

This book should be helpful for both aspiring and established leaders, in organizations of all sizes, who want to get more out of their team. But it is also for those who are not a team leader (yet) but a member of a team. Although team leaders have a strong impact on the teams they lead, each member of the team also has a role to play. Being a team member is too often ignored in the available resources on teams; it's as if everything depends solely on the team leader! Members can take it on themselves to find ways to work better together. Being a great member of a team is probably the most important skill for any future leader!

I will illustrate the key concepts and ideas I have developed with examples of actual teams with whom I have worked. They are not super teams. They have not climbed Mount Everest. They are normal, probably average, teams that have put small changes into place, and in doing so have grown and become more effective. When you read this book, you will hopefully recognize your own situation in the examples, and you will realize that your teams are in a place from which they can grow and evolve. Not by trying to emulate the 0.01% of super teams that other articles or business books write about, but by seeing that your team's situation is not so different from most others, and that you can take small steps to improve it. The target is for your teams to continuously grow and do better, moving towards higher performance. Whatever the current state of your team, you can make a real difference in your organization's performance and in your own legacy through your team's development.

THE UNTAPPED POTENTIAL OF TEAMS

Why developing a high-performance
team should excite you

TEAMS ALL AROUND

According to talent development leaders Andre Martin and Vidula Bal's white paper on the state of teams, 91% of employees and executives believe that teams are central to their organization's success, and leadership training company The Ken Blanchard Companies (qtd. in Andreatta) reports that 90% of employees say they spend a third or up to half of each day working in teams. Even Steve Jobs, who is not known for focusing on the people side of running a business, said, "Great things in business are never done by one person. They're done by a team of people." When investors evaluate a business preparing for an IPO, they will first and foremost look at the numbers.

But other elements come into consideration, and 90% of investors think the quality of the management team is the single most important non-financial factor when evaluating an IPO, according to Scott Keller and Mary Meaney in their book on leading organizations.

Teams are everywhere, and everyone is part of one or more teams at some point in their career. Teams vary in lifespan, geographic dispersion, and scope of work. They can be small, shop-floor manufacturing units or research teams spanning the globe. Of the organizational and leadership topics covered most consistently by *Harvard Business Review* between 1976 and 2016, high-performing leadership teams is ranked eighth out of 20 topics. Very few organizations, whatever field they operate in, would not list "teamwork" or "collaboration" as one of their core values.

Yet, when looking for examples of high-performance teams, we more often come across stories about sports teams or adventure teams, rather than teams in organizations. Zooming in on organizations, the great examples rarely come from the top. In the 2018 Global Human Capital Trends report by Deloitte, 51% of respondents rate C-suite collaboration as very important, yet 73% said their C-suite leaders rarely, if ever, work together on projects or strategic initiatives.

Are teamwork and collaboration part of your organization's values or ambitions? What are you doing to build teams and collaboration on a regular basis?

IT IS ALL ABOUT (SUSTAINED) PERFORMANCE

The term high-performance team is thrown around easily and a sense of "feel-good" or "band-of-best-buddies" often gets associated with such teams. A team where everybody feels as being among friends and where everyone has fun together for sure sounds better than the opposite. But that is not what a high-performance team is about: the focus should be on the "performance" part of the term.

The only raison d'être of a team is if it can as a whole make better decisions, innovate faster, and react better to the challenges it faces than the individuals making up the team would be able to alone. If these tasks can be successfully completed independently, there is no reason to spend time and energy on developing a team.

Imagine a team where team members fully engage with one another. Where they challenge but also support the others in the team. Where difficult issues are discussed and resolved. Where agreement reached during team meetings remains intact when the team members are not together. Where targets are built, and results are owned by the team members. Where each team member feels they contribute to the team's success and are enhanced by working with those around them. This is a team that truly performs on a high level and that will impact the organization to which it belongs.

" Nobody's perfect. But a team can be. "
– Meredith Belbin,
researcher and management consultant

A high-performance team needs to deliver on expectations, not for a few quarters or even a few years, but in a truly sustained way. If results and performance are the only things that are valued and discussed in a team, the team climate becomes cut-throat and threatening, and exhaustion and burnout can follow. A high-performance team keeps on delivering and maintains a positive and collaborative team climate despite the challenges coming its way.

How would your organization perform differently if you were able to build a high-performance team? How would your own work change?

TAKING TEAMS FOR GRANTED

Despite the omnipresence of teams, most professional development effort is focused on individuals. Coaching, mentoring, executive development programs (in-house or public), and most training programs are about developing the skills and competencies of each participant. We believe that people need to be trained, developed, and coached for them to become leaders, and we have plenty of approaches to make that happen. When it comes to teamwork, we seem to assume that putting all these well-trained and well-coached leaders together will result in a well-functioning team. That is not always the case. We do not really have a list of approaches to help teams develop and grow successfully.

Maybe it is because pretty much anyone in any culture has been familiar with teams since a very young age. Children join sports teams, youth groups, art classes, or music ensembles, which are great settings to help them develop socially and interact with others. We teach children that working together with and helping others are important. Cheering on professional sports teams or supporting successful music bands is popular all around the world. We celebrate teams that do well and become champions. We assume that since everyone knows what a team is about, everyone then more or less knows how a team functions, how to be part of a team, or how to lead one. When we start a professional career, we become part of a team, and we have all experienced that some teams work well and others don't. When we are assigned to a team or become part of a team in a work situation, we don't ask too many questions about how things will go. It could be because we all know what teams are about, or because our expectations of being part of a team are not very high. When a new initiative is announced, people get excited and have plenty of questions and concerns. Yet when someone is invited or told to be part of a team, questions or concerns either don't exist or are not expressed. Often, teams do not live up to expectations or to their potential. Ask people about their experiences with teams and they will more often share anecdotes about negative experiences than stories of high performance. They might recall an annual retreat or refer to the team's monthly meeting. Real conflict is probably (hopefully!) rare, but what we call a team is most of the time just a group of individuals coming together occasionally to share updates. A high-performance team is so much more. But you cannot get there without some effort.

> We think everybody knows what teams are about.
> But teams need development too.
> – Peter Cauwelier

Building up real collaboration and being part of a high-performance team should in fact be profoundly transformational for all involved, whether they are young recruits or senior leaders. The reality of teams in organizations is often a far cry from this potential. There is a major gap between our teams in organizations and the successful sports teams or music bands we idealize.

Maybe the best way to find out how much potential is left unexplored is to ask the team members themselves. In a survey of thousands of teams around the world,

Team Coaching International found that only 10% rate themselves in the zone of high-performance. Another survey by Korn Ferry and Harvard University found that 75% of 127 high-level teams were rated as mediocre or poor when evaluating whether the team accomplished big goals or grew more effective over time, and whether team members developed into better leaders. Although these are somber statistics, it is actually good news, because in most situations, very little genuine and sustained effort has been put into developing teams or helping people to be part of a team. Imagine the potential if your organization makes team development a priority and transforms just half of its teams into high-performance teams.

How would you rate the teams in your organization on the high-performance scale? And how would the team members themselves rate the teams they are part of? What if your organization's teams become known for achieving big goals and get recognized as the platform on which all your key players develop and grow?

WORKING WITH THE TEAM YOU HAVE

A chain is only as strong as its weakest link. Anything that is too heavy for that link will break it, and therefore the chain. This metaphor is often used to think about teams, where the overall performance of the team is constrained by the strength of the weakest team member. What do we do with the weakest member of the team? Train them?

Coach them? Fire and replace them? Whatever you do, once the weakest link is no longer the weakest… another member of the team takes its place. And so, we repeat.

The majority of people think they are better than average when it comes to driving a car, and most professionals would rate themselves above average in terms of their skills, competencies, or contributions to the team. This is known as the above-average effect or superiority bias. In the same vein, these professionals think that those they recruit into their team are in the top of the range—or at least well above the average—in terms of skills and competency: who would not want to have the very best candidate out there joining their team? The reality of the law of averages is that most of the members you hire into your team are closer to the average when it comes to their skills and competencies: not everyone can only be recruiting star players!

> " Despite your best recruitment efforts,
> you have far more average performers than
> A-players on your team. "
> – Peter Cauwelier

Thinking that you hire only those who are in the top 10% is very disconnected from reality. The real question then becomes: what can you do with a team of average players?

IT'S THE CONNECTIONS THAT MAKE THE DIFFERENCE

The good news is that a team of A-players rarely make up a high-performance team. It is the connections between your team members, however average they individually may be, that makes the difference in a team and determines a team's performance. It is not the "who" that makes the difference. It is the "how" that determines if your team is a high-performance team. Shannon Banks, Managing Director of Be Leadership and former Microsoft leadership development expert, highlights that despite the extreme level of connectivity we have achieved, "We are very connected to people from far away but disconnected from those near to us." In her leadership framework she emphasizes the need to move from connectivity to connections. The importance of connections has been confirmed in the famous Grant Study at Harvard Medical School as discussed by Professor George Vaillant in his book: meaningful relationships at work are the key to overall happiness. So, it is not just about "who" is on your bus, but more about what the connections between those who are on the bus look like.

> " The team is the connections. "
> – Peter Cauwelier

When a professional is let go from an organization, it is rarely because of lack of skills or competency. There are a plethora of ways to develop these at any level. When a professional fails, it is most often because that person cannot effectively work with or through others. When the CEO is fired, it is rarely because the strategy was wrong but rather because he was not able to get buy-in from the key stakeholders (the board, the executive team, etc.) and therefore failed to execute the strategy successfully. The team leader who is adored by everyone cannot make the difficult decisions and is stuck when the going gets tough. The peer whom everyone avoids because she is impossible to work with will at some point be asked to "look for other opportunities". When professionals fail, it is not because of the "what" or "who" but much more about "how" they work with and through others; it is because of the poor quality of the connections they developed with those around them. As investigative reportor Nicholas Carlson reveals in his book on her, when Marissa Mayer became CEO of Yahoo!, her decision to end the remote working policies was very unpopular. She pushed through because she was convinced that to really collaborate, team members needed to develop connections which could not take root only through technology: "To become the absolute best place to work, communication and collaboration will be important, so we need to be working side-by-side."

The real potential of your team is in the connections between the team members. What happens when the quality manager is adversely impacted by a new process the finance manager is proposing? Are they sitting down to find the best overall solution for the organization? Or does each stay within their respective areas of responsibility complaining about the other's lack of cooperation? Or even worse... does nothing happen until things go wrong and the leader must intervene? What would your team look like if all the connections worked optimally? If all your team members, with their individual strengths and weaknesses, communicate effectively, support one another, motivate one another, compensate for one another's gaps, or step in when someone is struggling, your team's performance will by far exceed the strength of the weakest—and even of the strongest—member! It is by working on the connections between team members that you will grow your team, not through the endless cycle of identifying and replacing the weakest link.

TEAMS ARE YOUR REAL HUMAN CAPITAL

At some point, you have probably hired away someone from another organization. You expect that bringing that new person into your organization will bring new talent, ideas, and energy. And that is obviously the case. But anyone can also hire away a member of your team. Then you are the one losing the talent, ideas, and energy. Human capital is defined as "the skills, knowledge, and experience possessed by an individual or population, viewed in terms of their value or cost to an organization or country". If your human talent pool is your strategic advantage, your competition can easily chip away at that advantage. It is different when your human capital is built on the principle of high-performance teams. Maybe a competitor can steal a team member, but it is unlikely they will hire away your entire team.

> " The truth is you don't need the best people,
> you need the best teams. "
> – Greg Satell, speaker, adviser, and author

Human capital is really only built when your focus is on developing teams by bringing together talented individuals. If the new marketing manager, with her talent, ideas, and energy, is only focusing on the marketing role, her talent and ideas will only benefit the marketing function. If your team is a high-performance team, the talent, ideas, and energy of the new marketing manager will be combined with and enhanced by the talent, ideas, and energy of the others in the team. The team, and by extension the organization, gets more than just the talent, ideas, and energy of the new member. The marketing manager's idea for a new campaign will be enhanced and made more robust by input from the other managers in the team. At the same time, the operations manager will expand his own experience by collaborating with the new marketing manager. A high-performance team multiplies and enhances the talents each of the team members brings with them. Of course, when someone leaves a high-performance team, there still is a negative impact, but that should not stop you from trying to develop such a team in the first place and build up real human capital.

CONCLUSION

Before you think about taking action and implementing ideas to develop a team, you need to be clear about why you would do so. If you are not convinced about the impact and benefit of team development, it is unlikely that you will manage to sustain your efforts amidst the challenges you will come across. If you are wondering what can really be gained from spending your energy on developing a team into a high-performance team, remember that:

- Teams are everywhere
- A high-performance team is all about performance
- We have often neglected to develop teams because there are no simple approaches
- Most of the members of your team are average, but the key is in the connections
- High-performance teams create a multiplier effect on your human capital

THE REALITY

THE PROBLEM WITH "MY TEAM"

Organizations typically proclaim teamwork or collaboration as part of their core values. Every leader or team member would be excited to be part of a high-performance team. Yet various realities of the work environment are not conducive to team development, or even radically obstruct it.

Ask any professional about teams and they will tell you about "their team". For the CEO it would be the team of VPs that report directly to him. The marketing director would talk about the marketing team. The production supervisor would refer to the different line leaders that report to her. If she has 15 direct reports, then that is "her team", all connected to her through neat reporting lines in the organization chart. What are these "teams" really doing when all the team members are together? Most often, the team will be reviewing progress or status updates, or listening to business updates. These team meetings can be led by the team leader, or team members can take turns to share updates about whatever falls in their scope of responsibilities.

This is not what teamwork is about. First of all, this is not really work since no specific result or output is created. At most, each member walks away from the session with a new understanding and awareness of what is going on in the organization. At worst, reporting or update meetings have no impact at all. Bringing "your team" together to look through PowerPoint slides or listen to the leader's or other team members' monologues is not a team at work. Secondly, of all the members in the room at that moment, the team leader is often the only one concerned with and following up on all the topics. The finance manager might be interested to get an update about how a recent customer issue was resolved, but this information will hardly impact his work. Most likely, he will not even share these updates with his own team, thinking it is not necessary—and maybe even distracting—for their work.

A team's purpose or reason for existence is not to share updates and information. There are plenty of tools for that and they probably are more effective than having lots of people sitting in a meeting room or joining online sessions for hours on end.

You may have 15 direct reports, and this may be clearly shown on the organization chart. But the organization chart shows people in boxes and reporting lines, not teams or team dynamics. And not all actual teams show up on the organization chart. In an article in the *Harvard Business Review*, Marcus Buckingham and Ashley Goodall point out that around half of the teams that exist at different levels in an organization are not visible on the organization chart. These teams are the result of personal initiatives, where members of the organization motivated by a specific goal come together to make things happen.

Fifteen people cannot be a team. Research has shown that the optimum size for a team is six to seven members with a suggested minimum at five and a maximum at nine. If the team

REALITY
You have too many direct reports for a team.

is too small, there is not enough diversity of experience and ideas, and a single person leaving the team has such a great impact that it can bring the team to a halt. The tendency is more often to have too many members in a team than too few. When we are looking at creating a team, we typically think, "Who else could or should we add to the team?" Sometimes, when we invite one person to be on the team, we also have to invite another to avoid creating discontent. Having too many members in a team brings its own set of challenges. First and foremost is the logistical difficulty of scheduling meeting times that work for everyone. When there are too many team members, there will be a trend for sub-teams to develop, with different views and incomplete alignment with the team overall. Large groups also allow for social loafing or free riding: when several team members are pulling their weight, some others may get away with doing as little as possible. Cohesion and sense of team outside of the actual team meetings or working sessions are difficult to maintain.

Think of the last time you were in a meeting with more than 10 people. What was everyone doing? It is very unlikely that all were contributing, listening, suggesting, and collaborating to create a common result or outcome. In all likelihood, a few individuals were taking up all the airtime, a few more were interested but hesitant to participate due to their status or because they felt overpowered by others, and the rest were biding their time waiting for the meeting to end so they could get "back to work"!

IT'S NOT JUST ABOUT THE TEAM MEMBERS

Leaders talking about their team sometimes explain they have a great team except for the marketing manager. Or the human resources manager. Or another manager. If only they could replace that particular team member with the perfect marketing, human resources, or other manager, then all would be well. Finding someone new takes time, is costly, and however great someone's CV, resume, or LinkedIn profile may look, the reality is always more nuanced. Even if the perfect candidate is found, there is no guarantee that this new member will work well with the others on the team. There are plenty of examples of sports superstars who moved to another team and then didn't perform nearly as well. These star players did not lose their individual skills overnight; they didn't connect with the others on the team and therefore didn't perform.

Leaders often think that they need the best on their team. When we interview someone to fill a vacant position in a team, we—explicitly or not—rate the candidates on a scale and compare them with the other candidates and the people already on the team. We will look for the "best" person from all the candidates we evaluate. When we settle on the final choice, we are convinced that this person is the best of all the ones we have looked at. Next time we need to interview someone for another position, we again will try and find the best person out there. So, we build a team of the "best" players by selecting the best of the pool of available candidates each time we recruit. Once the new hire is on board, we create an introduction program where she will spend some time with all her peers. After getting to know one another, sharing professional experiences, and some chitchatting, the new hire is more or less ready to be a full-fledged and effective team member! The development of the connections that will really impact the team dynamics and performance, are left up to luck or happenstance.

A few weeks or months down the road, it turns out that the new hire is more "average" than initially thought.

> **REALITY**
> Focus is on the individuals instead of the team as a whole.

It's not that this new team member has told blatant lies during the interviews, or that a skill or experience she declared does not exist. And anyhow, it is rare for someone not to perform well professionally because he or she cannot master a certain skill. Organizations have all kind of support or training to help fill critical skill gaps. Most of the time, what starts to go wrong—very slowly at first—is how this new team member is connecting with the others in the team. According to Byford, Watkins, and Triantogiannis in an article in the *Harvard Business Review*, 57% of senior executives joining a new team say that a major stumbling block and potential derailer for their career is the difficulty of forging alliances with peers.

In what he termed the super-chicken experiment, William Muir from Purdue University studied two separate groups of chickens over two chicken generations. The first group of average chickens laying average-sized eggs was left to evolve naturally: chickens were born, grew up, and in turn, laid their eggs. The size of the group was kept constant by removing at random the excess number of chickens at each generation. This was a group of average chickens laying average-sized eggs. After two generations, the productivity of this group—measured by the size of the eggs produced—had increased by 20%, and each chicken seemed to live happily alongside the others. In the second group, only the super-chickens were kept in the group—the biggest and strongest chickens that produced the largest eggs. In this group, the total number of chickens was kept constant by removing the smaller chickens or the ones that laid the smallest eggs. Each new generation, only super-chickens continued to populate the group. After two generations of breeding and keeping only super-chickens, the productivity of the second group drastically dropped. Why? The super-chickens—becoming larger, more aggressive, more "super" with each generation—ended up fighting for dominance and killing off many of the competing super-chickens in the group. Although it was comprised of the biggest and strongest chickens, the group had pretty much been decimated, resulting in fewer eggs.

The super-chicken experiment has interesting parallels with how we manage individuals and teams in organizations. We assess, hire, promote, and reward mostly based on individual performance and skills, yet expect that these high-performance individuals will then work effectively as a team. In her TED talk, Margaret Heffernan argues that building a strategy on finding only the best will often backfire. Does it make sense to try and identify the "best" individual performer to join a team or to promote to a higher level of responsibility? In fact, is it possible to have a high-performance team where everyone is a star? In their book on organizational culture, Robert Kegan and Lisa Lahey reveal that Next Jump, an e-commerce company, used to look for high performers when recruiting new members, until they realized what this approach led to: "We recruited for similar characteristics that others do—for who was the smartest, the most driven. We looked for the most competitive and driven people. We ended up hiring what we later called 'brilliant jerks'".

We spend so much time and effort on getting the best people to join our team, yet then hope the rest will just happen by itself. It is how the team members work together that determines whether the team becomes a high-performance team or just a group of super-members each trying to be the biggest of the pack. It is the quality of the connections that determines the level of the team collaboration and performance, more than the quality of the individual team members.

WHEN THE CAT'S AWAY

When I ask leaders what happens when they are not around, they tell me that things are working just fine, and that work moves along and gets done as it should be. Thank God for that, but is that really where your expectations of your team should end? That the routine stuff gets done? That team members stay in their comfort zones and stick to their established work habits? What happens when something important and out of the routine comes up?

> **REALITY**
> Your team only deals with routine work when you're not around.

When an issue requires joint action or decisions, and the team leader is not around, does your team get together, come up with solutions, and decide on the best way forward? Or do they get lost in arguments and turf wars, and develop workarounds or duplicate work to avoid dealing with the issue head-on? Do they stay in their comfort zone (a.k.a. job title, department, or small circle of buddies within the team) or do they take the risk of stepping up and finding a solution, even if it is "not their job"? Or—and this is probably what happens most often—is the issue put on the "pending" list waiting for your return? It seems that only routine work gets done when the team leader is not around to make the decisions.

When you are not around, the "team" that you visualize when you think about the group of your direct reports will often disintegrate back into its discrete components. The human resources manager will go and focus on human resources priorities, and the marketing person will focus on the marketing assignment you handed out. The team ceases to exist when the team leader is not holding it together; when the cat's away, the mice are not playing around but go in hibernation. That may boost the leader's ego and perceived importance, but that is not what a high-performance team is about.

COMMUNICATING IS NOT COLLABORATING

Many tools market themselves as collaboration tools and new ones pop up all the time. Always-on applications allow unlimited numbers of people to connect and share information. But are these tools really supporting collaboration? It is useful to distinguish communication from collaboration.

Communication is exchanging information. With modern tools and apps, I can communicate with hundreds of people at the same time. But getting a "read" confirmation or even a "like" in Line or WhatsApp does not mean anything but that. It does not mean, "I received your message, understood it, and will act on it." Although modern communication tools claim to replace old ones like email, not much has really changed. Meetings where each team member presents a status update to others are also forms of communication, not collaboration.

REALITY
Communicating is not collaborating.

Coordinating, cooperating, and collaborating are terms that are thrown around easily and interchangeably, yet they are in fact very different, and it is useful to identify which of these three levels of work you need within your team. Coordinating is sharing information to support and align distinct actions to allow individuals to reach distinct goals. Coordination produces efficiency but members and their tasks remain independent from the others. Cooperation is when members perform their assigned part of an agreed-upon shared process or task. Each depends on the others to reach the shared objective. Finally, collaboration is about co-creating to reach a shared goal or vision, where the result or outcome is changed by the input of and the interaction between the contributors. As Britt Andreatta states in her book *Wired to Connect* on the neuroscience behind teams, the contributions by team members are interdependent, with each unique contribution critical to the whole. Ask yourself whether your teams are collaborating or just communicating.

TOO LITTLE TIME (FOR EVERYTHING)

Any leader would agree that learning is important. Organizations and teams need to learn to better deal with the more and more complex business challenges of our time. We should learn all the time so that our next sales meeting, project review, or one-on-one discussion is better than the last one. Without learning, we are stuck in the treadmill-like busy-ness of doing things, repeating those things, and then doing some more things. And then we wonder why we struggle to create breakthrough performance.

Though we invest a lot in leadership and team development, or learning in general, there remains a disconnect between the learning and the actual work. When we think of learning, we think of the training room, the off-site development program, or the MBA cohort.

> **REALITY**
> We are so busy but have no time to learn.

In the office, we... work! There are so many priorities to deal with that we do not really have much time to go for training or learning sessions. Because when we are in training sessions, the work does not get done. Moreover, we know that, despite all the great insights from the training sessions, very few manage to apply the new learning in their work. And yet we stick to the traditional way of learning and developing, disconnected from the actual work. Because the traditional kind of learning and development interferes with work, it takes place only when we have some spare time (and funds).

THE TEAM IS YOUR LIMIT

You may be a great leader with great experience, the perfect strategic vision, and a brilliant plan of what your team should focus on. But your team is your limit, not the sky, although that's what consultants sometimes make you believe.

Consultants dazzle you with the best practices or state-of-the-art developments that other organizations out there achieve. You feel pretty embarrassed that your organization

> **REALITY**
> The team is your limit.

has not yet achieved what everyone else apparently has been doing for ages. Clearly all the other leaders out there (and their teams) are way ahead. If only you can replicate what the consultant offers up, your organization will reach new heights.

Consultants do not consider your team. Of course, there will be a "change management" component included in the program, with a gap analysis and a few go-live training sessions. But this approach does not take into account the team members' skills, connections, or experiences; it focuses on the processes, culture, or knowledge (whatever the subject of the intervention is). In the end, the consultants will move on and leave you and your team behind. The extent to which the processes, culture, or knowledge will change following the consultant's intervention, depends on your team.

That is why so many consulting interventions—or other grand plans—end up fizzling out or fail to deliver the incredible gains that were promised. An organization performs through its teams. Consultants can bring their expertise and experience from other missions. But if the change or improvement initiative is not built with your team at the core of the change or improvement, disappointment (including frustration and finger-pointing) is guaranteed. You may have great vision and the best strategy, but it is your team that determines the extent to which your vision and strategy is turned into success.

YOU HAVE THE TEAM YOU DESERVE!

REALITY
Your team is a reflection of you as a leader.

Philosopher Joseph de Maistre said that nations get the government they deserve. In the same vein, your team is the one you deserve. Except for a team leader inheriting a new team for the first couple of months, your team is the reflection of you as a leader. Team leaders sometimes vent about their teams: team members don't have the needed skills, don't take responsibility, are not decisive, or stay in their comfort zone.

But what is the team leader doing about all this? Have they coached, mentored, given feedback, or reacted when things improved or did not improve? Are there clear targets and a clear understanding of what happens when targets are not met? If the answer is yes to all this and the expected results are still not reached, what is the leader going to do differently next week? The team leader who is not satisfied with certain situations but doesn't do anything about them (other than venting) or gives up, is sending through his inaction a very clear message to the team about his priorities and values.

The results of developing a high-performance team also reflect on the team leader once they have moved on. The team someone leaves behind is an important part of their legacy. The new products, services, or strategic acquisitions the leader managed will be dated and forgotten not long after moving on. But what about the team? Does the team continue to perform as a high-performance team even when the leader is no longer there? Or does the successor have to start all over and clean shop in the first 90 days to get all the losers off the bus? As Florian Kratz's article in *Fortune* tells us, Jack Welch's legacy spread far beyond General Electric when several members of his leadership team moved on to take leadership positions in other Fortune 100 companies. Paul Watzlawick said that you cannot not communicate. In the same way, you cannot not build your team. How a leader deals with the team challenges that they are facing, what the team they leave behind looks like, and how team members and others talk about the leader, is how that leader will be remembered.

CONCLUSION

Being convinced about the potential of developing a high-performance team is a necessary condition to that development. Unfortunately, for many who are either in leadership positions or members of a team, their experience and the realities in which they operate frequently do not create the right conditions or stimulus to make developing high-performance teams a priority. For most team leaders and teams, the reality is that:

- You have too many direct reports for a team
- The focus is on the development of the individuals, not of the team as a whole
- Your team stays in its comfort zone doing routine work when you are not around to prioritize or make decisions
- Although we all communicate more and more, collaborating remains hard work
- Everybody is so busy that learning often doesn't make the priority list
- Despite your talents and efforts, your team is your limit
- Except for the first couple of months, the team you have with all its strengths and issues is a reflection of you

PART TWO

BUILDING, DEVELOPING, AND GROWING Teams

In Part Two, we will look at how to build a new team or re-build an existing team, and how to grow it towards a level of sustained high performance.

First, we meet James, an imaginary character who is a composite of managers and leaders I have met. James is a successful professional who takes on a job as managing director with Widgets International. We find out about the challenges he encounters in his first 18 months and how he deals with them. James has great energy, solid experience, and good intentions, but after a year and a half and lots of energy spent, he is not at the level of success he had expected for himself.

Part Two then gets concrete about building a new team or re-building an existing team. We look at how the number of members impacts a team's efficiency, remind ourselves of the very simple yet often overlooked basics of managing a team and their importance, discover how learning within a team develops its connections, learn the impact of identifying team goals, roles, and norms, and finally, discuss how recruitment can become a way to set a team up for success. These different concepts are illustrated by practical examples of how teams can implement these elements.

Once these basic elements are solidly in place and maintained, the next level in team development tackles how to grow a team, and in particular how building up psychological safety in the team sets it up for permanent learning and sustained performance. The key components of team psychological safety are building real mutual support, making asking for help a normal practice, tackling complex issues, and reacting smartly to mistakes. The importance of these components is explained in detail and illustrated with concrete and actionable techniques that have benefited many teams. Finally, we look at how we can apply the notion of practice to a team; after all, sports or other inspiring teams spend most of their time practicing before they get to the actual performance.

A TALE OF TWO TEAMS: JAMES

James finally had a long weekend all to himself and decided to get away and spend some time in a resort on the beach. It had been a hectic 18 months since he joined Widgets International as Managing Director. He felt somewhat burnt out and yet it seemed like so much still needed to be done. What was going wrong?

It had been a great start when he was hired by the CEO to lead the organization. His impressive LinkedIn CV, numerous testimonials, and track record of getting things done had put him on top of the shortlist of candidates. His negotiation skills had succeeded in squeezing out a better compensation package than Widgets International had initially proposed. He had been brought in to set things back on track after a lackluster three years under the previous managing director.

The first days were pretty cool, meeting all the key people at the headquarters. There had been lots of talks with his leadership team, during which he tried to assess each of them quickly for potential. Within five minutes of talking with the sales manager, he already knew she would be the first one out! Her conservative attitude drove him crazy just talking to her, and he could not imagine having to work with her at all! The others in the team seemed pretty average and he clearly saw his work cut out.

The first task he gave to the human resources manager was to get rid of the sales manager and find a results-focused go-getter as soon as possible. James interviewed the top three and within one month the new sales manager was on board! The human resources manager had expressed a preference for another candidate, but on this James went with his instincts and he was excited that his leadership team was finally ready.

James had quickly put in place the familiar routines that he knew were part of his success in the past. He set up a bimonthly review meeting with all 15 members of his leadership team. Each was asked to apply a standard format to their presentation slides because that would build a sense of uniformity and professionalism. The large conference room was blocked for two hours every other Tuesday and he ran a tight meeting, staying on track and on target. James was a big believer in Peter Drucker's key idea that "you can't manage what you can't measure." He asked probing questions to find out why certain indicators were not moving in the right direction. At first the team members seemed a bit rattled by his proactive style, but they quickly got used to it and prepared their presentations flawlessly. Each shared their update and received input from James on how to solve the issues they encountered. James was a bit disappointed that there was little participation from the others but then again, he was the only one with the overall view and vision of where Widgets International needed to move towards. It was only normal that as captain of the ship he oversaw everything. After each presentation was finished and he had asked his questions or made his comments, James always asked if anyone else had any questions (he had heard learned that in a leadership course a while ago). But there were never any and it seemed everyone was clear about everything, so they would then move on to the next presenter.

In addition to the team meeting, James regularly called the team members individually into his office. For this there was no schedule, and it really depended on the priorities of the moment. You cannot plan out everything and then expect things to follow the plan! Leaders need to be flexible and ready to react whenever called upon. He knew not all the members of the leadership team liked this approach. A few seemed to enjoy the exchange and eagerly listened to James' ideas and suggestions. Some seemed to use the meeting just to complain about others, whether it was members of their own team or peers from the leadership team. Each time James had to take note and follow up with the other peer. It seemed these leaders could not really get much done without him pointing out the way or making the decisions. And with a few others, it was really a pain to get anything out of them, so James soon avoided dealing with them and went directly to their team members. You can only try so many times!

James was a big believer in making sure everyone on the team had all the information available. He had put in place a shared document filing system where he regularly added resources. Several times a day, he sent out emails to the entire leadership team so they were up to date with everything that was going on and could take any initiative necessary.

He had been given a free hand by the CEO in redressing Widget International's performance so had not hesitated to call upon the consulting company that he had worked with in his previous role. The consultant team had analyzed the accounts, interviewed each member of the leadership team, and after three weeks of intense diagnosis, revealed an ambitious plan that would turn Widget International around in only 12 months. James had been super excited but was disappointed by his leadership team's rather neutral reactions. He had wondered why they could not see the great potential for the company. Anyway, James had managed to convince the CEO that this was the solution to all of Widget International's ills, and he had gotten his vote of confidence! Only three months into the job and he was ready to create another success story. He decided to take the lead role in executing the plan and assigned tasks based on his leadership team's individual roles and responsibilities. He followed up on each task with a detailed reporting system and led a review meeting each month with the team.

He had also asked the human resources manager to organize a team-building weekend away from the office. A bit of a waste of time in his opinion but someone had brought it up once and it seemed the leadership team thought this was a good idea. It actually turned out to be great fun and everybody seemed really relaxed. The leadership team was divided up into small groups and went through several creativity and collaboration challenges. There was the spaghetti tower-building competition (he had done this before, so he showed his group how and of course they won the competition!) and lots of exchanges about high-performance teams!

At the end of James' first year at Widgets International, the operations manager left the company, which didn't really help things. James had a long exit interview with the manager to find out why he was leaving, but he just said he had found another job. James tried to fish for useful information about issues with the other members of the leadership team but there was not much forthcoming. The operations manager's peers didn't seem too concerned about him leaving. The team meetings were not really any different. James had to take on the operations manager's main tasks, so that added to his overall workload. He had hoped that the engineering manager would be able to take on some of the tasks, but she said she was not familiar with what the operations manager did.

It was crazy how the last 18 months had flown by. James was not really happy about how things were going. There were some positives but Widgets International had not delivered on the plan he had proposed to the CEO. The main key performance indicators were lagging, and in their recent exchanges, the CEO seemed a bit less enthusiastic about what was going on in the organization. There was no denying that a few new product launches had not delivered, and two key clients had moved to another supplier. And top of that, James was tired. It was time for some drastic action.

After some reflection, James was clear on what needed to be done! He would first of all call back the consulting team to identify why the ambitious plan was not successful. He also decided to increase the frequency of the team meeting to every week so he could discover any issue or deviation from the plan more quickly. Finally, he would also hire a headhunter to find a new human resources manager. He had tolerated him for way too long.

BUILDING AND DEVELOPING YOUR TEAM

What are the basics?

START NOW, WHENEVER THAT IS

When is the best time to start working on your team's development? That question came up at a team session with a team that was newly formed following a regional reorganization in an Asian manufacturing company. This new team had been announced only two months earlier, and because not everybody was located in the same office, some team members had not yet met their new team peers (although they all knew one another). At the end of the first day of our two-day team session, one participant shared that it would have been better if they had more team history (six months or so) because this would make the workshop more effective. He changed his mind by the end of the second day.

All too often, leaders look for help with their team only when things start to go south. They begin to worry when people are getting entrenched

in their respective silos. They think about taking action when the team is treading water and not delivering on its targets and commitments. They look for change only when tensions or even conflicts arise. Of course, working on team dynamics in this situation can help, and collaboration and performance can improve. But there is no need to wait for a painful and urgent reason to start working on your team's development. When it comes to a team, the old saying, "When it ain't broke, don't fix it" does not apply!

Tuckman's team development model has been popular since the 1960s, and Tuckman declared that the forming, storming, norming, and performing stages are all necessary and inevitable in order for the team to grow, face up to challenges, tackle problems, find solutions, plan work, and deliver results. The storming phase is where tensions and conflicts arise. According to Tuckman's model, different working and communication styles impact the functioning of the team and these differences need to be worked out for the team to be able to progress. In reality, the storming phase can create lasting negative memories, and relationships remain forever impacted by how the tensions played out. Team members may rationally agree to "move on" but conflicts are rarely completely erased and forgotten.

Depending on the intensity of the storm, some team members can remain impacted by the clouds that continue to surround them for a long time, and this constrains the team. A vase that breaks into pieces can be glued together but will never be the same.

Contrary to Tuckman's premise, the storming phase can actually be avoided. The earlier you start to work on your team, the better it is. Day two of the team session mentioned earlier was built around responsibilities, a shared goal, and team norms. Team members shared their own targets and expressed what help they needed from whom. They then established the norms they would start to work with as a team. Finally, they identified one single project that they would jointly work on, and that would show their efficiency and impact as the organization's leadership team, both to themselves and to the rest of the organization. The team leader said at the end of the workshop: "Really happy we did this. We saved a lot of time!" Don't wait for storm clouds to appear to start working on your team! The best time to start developing your team is now.

KEEP IT SMALL

There are two elements to consider when thinking about the size of a team. The first is the number of members: a team of five, or seven, or nine. That is most often the key characteristic of the team and it is what the organization chart or the team's visual representation reflects. The second element to consider is the number of connections. A connection is the "linkage" between any two team members and represents their working relationship—"how" these two team members work together. Member A may have a great connection with member B and member B may have a great connection with member C, but this does not guarantee that members A and C have a great connection. When members A and B work together, all goes well. The same is true when members B and C work together. But when members A, B, and C sit down to work together on a particular task, things can be very different. The connections between pairs of members are also impacted by other connections nearby. It is all these connections that exist between the different team members that really determine the team dynamics and team potential.

In a team of nine people (including the team leader), there are eight leader-subordinate relationships. These relationships are a key element of the team dynamics. But these relationships only represent a small part of what is going on in this team. With nine people, there are in total 36 relationships, not just eight. The eight relationships around the team leader represent less than one-fifth of the relationships or connections in the team. The leader obviously plays a key role in a team, but even if he does an excellent job with the eight connections he is a part of, the reality of the team, and how

TIP

The ideal number of members in a team is six or seven.

it performs, is much more complex. As a leader, you may have developed trustworthy relationships with each of the people in your circle, but that does not automatically mean all these team members have equally trusting relationships with one another! There are two ways to look at the full picture of this team. The first is to say, "Wow, this is way too complex to even try to do anything about it." The second is to say, "Wow, look at all the potential in this team if all 36 connections and relationships were working optimally."

In a team with N members, there are N x (N-1)/2 connections or relationships. A team of five team members has ten connections. A team of eight team members has 28 connections. You have 15 direct reports in your "leadership team"? There are 105 connections in this team. Since it is not just about who is in the team (the team members) but much more about how these team members work together (the connections), it is clear that large teams cannot function properly. Some researchers put the absolute maximum of members in a team at 12, but most of them find that the limit is nine. And the "best" number of people in a team is six or seven.

Keep the number of people in a team as small as possible. The approach should be to bring together the smallest number necessary to provide the needed skills and perspectives to get the work done. With each member you plan to put on the team, explicitly ask yourself if the project cannot be completed without that person. Don't fall in the temptation of adding a few more people "just to be sure" or thinking that if we invite A, we also should invite B to the team to avoid them feeling upset. Maybe you have ten or 15 people in your team. These 15 direct reports may look like a solid unit on the organization chart, but they will never all work together. Not every one of these people should be involved in every project or challenge: it makes much more sense to create several distinct teams. Real collaboration works well with six or seven members. Rather than think about "your team" as what the organization chart displays, try to consider "your teams". When there is a new product launch, maybe only four or five of your team members need to be involved. When there is a corporate initiative that needs to be rolled out, another set of team members can take on that task. Those are your teams. There are probably several teams active at any given time, made up of members from your group of direct reports. They could form a team for a few days only, or for a few months. They work on a specific topic, trying to reach a particular goal or deal with a current challenge. They take the lead, communicate internally and externally with the relevant stakeholders, keep one another updated, and huddle when a decision needs to be made or a problem addressed. These teams can be officially mandated teams. You can appoint someone in charge of a subject, and that person will need to gather people to get things done. Or you can mandate a few people to be responsible: "John, Susan, and Angela will be in charge of the new IT implementation." You can have review or update meetings with all 15 direct reports, but the actual work gets done in sub-teams of fewer members.

GETTING THE BASICS OF TEAM MANAGEMENT RIGHT

At some point, entrepreneurs who have successfully grown their idea into a real business realize that their once one-person outfit has grown to an organisation of 20, 50, or even more people. They can no longer do everything themselves. They have grown their team, but they cannot afford to hire managers whose only job it is to manage others, as they are still very much relying on each individual's contribution to help grow the top line and keep the bottom line in check. They need to start acting as team leaders themselves. Newly promoted managers have a similar challenge, and there is not really a handbook readily available for them. Where do you concretely start when you need to lead a team?

Before looking at leading a team it is worthwhile to repeat the basics of managing a team, because often these are not fully and consistently implemented, even in established organizations. In addition, embedding learning within the team right from the start sets the team up for continuous progress.

1. **A Few Basic Indicators**

     Your team needs a few key performance indicators (KPI)—start with one!—that are critical to the business, that the members clearly understand, and that are visible to everyone at all times. The team should clearly see that its efforts and results impact this key indicator directly. The indicator needs to be up-to-date at all times, and if possible kept current by the team itself. There is nothing more demoralizing than a KPI display that has not been updated for months. There is no need to have walls full of charts; too many indicators become meaningless very quickly.

2. **Regular One-on-One Meetings**

The team manager should have a regular one-on-one meeting with each of the members of the team. This one-on-one meeting can be informal, over breakfast or lunch, but it must be

> **TIP**
> The basics are: key indicators, one-on -ones, and a regular team meeting.

clear it is a working meeting, and it should take place every two weeks at a minimum. It is a discussion to clarify what is going well and what is not, to identify what support is needed going forward, and to be clear and explicit when performance issues need to get addressed. A formal agenda or minutes are not really needed, but both sides need to come prepared with updates from the previous meeting as well as further issues to be discussed. The review can be about the progress on different ongoing topics, but also needs to look at the team member's well-being. How is she feeling in the team? Which of the tasks does she feel most motivated about? What is she struggling with? If any actions are decided, timing and ownership need to be clarified explicitly. This is also where the relationship (in other words connection) between the manager and the team member is developed and maintained. The meeting should be balanced, with ideally equal airtime for both sides. If the team manager is doing all the talking, explaining or clarifying, it is not a one-on-one meeting.

3. **A Regular Team Meeting**

    At regular intervals, the whole team should come together to review the organization's priorities, including the key indicators. The meeting should be guided and led by the manager, but team members should be encouraged to update one another, discuss options, make decisions, and help one another out where needed. The team meeting needs to focus on the team's overall performance and the synergies to be explored. At the initial stage, this meeting is more about fostering cooperation rather than collaboration. This kind of meeting can be a bit awkward at first, but the team manager should persist. These team meetings—when all the team members are together—are what creates the "image of the team" for the team members.

These three basic team building blocks are not a set from which to pick one or two. These basic elements are linked and need to co-exist. You can't have only one-on-one meetings (where talk often moves to complaints about the people who are not in the room) or only indicators on the wall (without a team review of the progress). In large organizations, there is often a plethora of indicators and meetings, but there is "no time" for genuine one-on-one discussions. Managers often have an inappropriate balance between one-on-one and team meetings. They are more comfortable with one or the other, and therefore focus on that element. A conscious effort is needed to establish and maintain all these basic elements to really set the team up for success.

These are simple steps that don't take up too much time, and they go a long way in providing direction, basic structure, and follow-up for your team. They are the basic steps of team development, and if a team manager cannot put them in place then there is no need to try and jump to the more advanced steps right away. Even for a team that has significantly progressed, the three basics of KPI, one-on-one meetings, and team meetings need to remain in place.

LEARNING AS A WAY OF WORKING

When thinking of learning in an organizational context, most think about the human resources function and their responsibility to run training programs. We think of learning as knowledge we receive from third parties whom we must pay for their services. Although this is a meaningful and important form of learning, not all learning falls under this category. The definition of learning is "the process of acquiring new, or modifying existing, knowledge, behaviors, skills, values, or preferences". From the definition, it is clear that learning does not require an external expert or an off-site venue.

> " Teams are a fundamental source
> of learning and organizational effectiveness.
> It is little wonder that the workplace of the 21st century
> places a premium on team-based learning. "
> – Amy C. Edmondson, Professor,
> Harvard Business School

To be meaningful and connected with work priorities, learning must be embedded in regular activities. A simple yet powerful way to explore all the dimensions of learning is through asking questions. Asking questions for which we know the answer is equivalent to a test, trying to check if the other person knows the correct answer as well. We do not learn from questions like this. Asking questions for which we don't have an answer is an inborn human skill that is the foundation of learning. At a very young age, children start to ask adults questions, because they assume the adults know more than they do. They don't ask their playmates because they know they won't know the answer either. They often ask very pure yet intriguing questions. They never ask questions to which they know the answer, to "test" if the adult knows the correct answer too. Unfortunately, that natural talent is very quickly suppressed in the education system where acquiring knowledge is not rooted in asking questions but reduced to remembering information that is taught. Those who remember the correct answer get awarded with higher grades. As Neil Postman and Charles Weingartner point out in their book on teaching, "The most important intellectual ability man has yet developed—the art and science of asking questions—is not taught in school!" Once adults join an organization, they are assessed not on the kind of learning questions they ask but rather on what they know and how well they can share that knowledge with others. The concept of learning has been disconnected from asking questions, and learning has now been reduced to absorbing knowledge while participating in corporate training programs. Rediscovering that most important tool of asking questions is a great way to genuinely learn and develop within the structure of a team, with direct and concrete benefits both for the team dynamics and connections, and for the team performance. A team is the perfect setting in which to learn about one another, learn from one another, and make learning an ever-present facet of the team's culture.

1. **Learning about One Another**

    The leader of the project management department in a multinational company shared that for him, the key to building a great team was for the team leader to know each member of the team very well, including their expectations and needs. I fully agree! But why would the need to really know others well be limited to the leader-subordinate connection? What about having all team members know one another very well, including their needs, preferences, and expectations? Asking questions is not only a great way to get to know newcomers to the team, but also to discover unknown dimensions of someone you have worked side-by-side with for several years. In a team, we often have very close relationships with a few of the team peers, even doing activities together outside of work. Yet for others we really only know their job title through sitting in on the same meetings. Creating dialogues based on questions allows us to get to know others better, both in terms of the work they do and their personal lives. Team members may discover that the only contribution of the accounting manager they are aware of—the monthly accounting report—actually requires different complex steps to reach the monthly closure. Some may find out that a colleague they work with has similar favorite pastimes. Asking genuine, curious questions and listening closely to what others share bring powerful benefits. As Andrew Sobel and

Jeroid Panas explain in their book on the power of questions, "Telling creates resistance, asking creates relationships."

Opening up about personal lives needs to be managed carefully and it cannot be forced upon people. Some are open about sharing personal experiences but for others this means really getting out of their comfort zone. But the foundation of building a team is mutual trust and you cannot build up trust with someone you do not know on a personal level, as Patrick Lencioni reveals in *Overcoming the Five Dysfunctions of a Team*. In every team learning session I have been part of, the participants appreciated the new things they learned about the others they work with. Sometimes conversations are intense and deep, in other situations there are bursts of laughter!

2. **Learning from One Another**

Rather than learning from an external guru or consultant, team members can have conversations about their practical experiences and develop shared insights. They can learn from one another and they can teach one another. A simple exercise is to ask team members to write down what they want to learn more about. They then display these learning needs somewhere everyone

TIP

Make learning between team members a key habit.

can see. All the other team members can offer their support if they think they can help the requester learn more about a particular aspect of the job. Getting stuck in routine work, we often don't have the time to see what we can learn from those nearest to us, or how we can share our knowledge with others in the team. "I never thought about this issue in the way she described her experience, and she gave me a very easy way to better deal with it in the future" was one testimony from a participant in one of my workshops. Singapore-based DBS Bank introduced a policy of teach-backs where anyone can sign up to get a scholarship to learn something new, on the condition that they then "teach back" within the organization what they have learned. Teaching something back to others is the best form of learning and at the top of the learning pyramid. Experts at all levels can be invited to share their knowledge and experience with others and be recognized for this.

Imagine all the knowledge and experience collectively held by all the members in your organization, and the possibilities and potential that could be unlocked if all this knowledge and experience were explored, shared, and acted upon.

> If only HP knew what HP knows,
> we would be three times more productive.
> – Lew Platt, CEO Hewlett-Packard

3. Learning All the Time

Learning should be a daily recurring process. As the pioneer of action learning Reg Revans states, "There is no learning without action and no action without learning." There are learning opportunities in every activity that is part of the workday, such as team meetings, client meetings, project reviews, one-on-one discussions, status updates, performance review meetings, or recruitment interviews. It is quite easy to create a habit of extracting learning in a deliberate way within team or one-on-one meetings. At the end of the meeting, ask team members what went well and what should be changed for the next session. Give your team some time to reflect and share their thoughts. When is the last time you asked them to reflect and share what they had learned? You might be surprised by the quality of what they share.

The World Institute for Action Learning (WIAL) describes action learning as a question-based team process explicitly focusing on solving complex problems and learning at the same time. At several moments in the discussion process, the team coach will invite the members to reflect and share about what they are learning, either about themselves, about others in the team, or about the challenge under discussion. It is very powerful to go around the group and ask each member what they have learned, how they see this experience, how it changes their view of the situation, and how they will act upon this new learning.

Training and development programs are of course valuable. If you want to reward your team or take some relaxing time off, by all means have fun in the outdoors with a team-building exercise. But these only contribute in a very small way to what a team needs to learn and grow. There is a lot of potential within the team itself that can be fully explored on the path to becoming a high-performance team. You don't build teams by taking them out of their context and doing things that are disconnected or even opposite to their role in the organization. You build teams by supporting people to learn and work together.

CREATING THE TEAM FRAMEWORK

Once the basics are in place—and remain in place—a team can build up three more advanced building blocks to take a step up towards higher performance: a team goal, clear roles, and team norms.

1. **A Team Goal**

    A team goal is a shared goal that the team agrees upon and works towards. It is amazing how teams often have a multitude of individual goals for each team member (or department) but no real shared goal. "Growing revenue by X%" is often

> **TIP**
> Set a team goal, clear roles, and team norms (and follow up).

seen as the goal for the business development division and the procurement team may not feel they have any role to play in it. "Reducing costs" is handled by the procurement or operations department and the human resources department may feel this does not apply to them.

Teams should set up both task goals and process goals. Task goals involve the usual metrics or KPI mentioned earlier around business imperatives like profit, number of clients, quality improvements, or customer satisfaction. Process goals concern the team itself and are about how the team works, decides, or communicates. For example, when a team is struggling to make decisions within expected timeframes, it could create the shared process goal of "making critical decisions impacting the organization within two weeks and using not more than four team meetings".

A shared goal should be one the entire team feels ownership and responsibility towards; it is not delegated to just a few team members. It should be SMART (specific, measurable, ambitious, relevant, and time-bound), and should be explicit and communicated to the rest of the organization. The team works on it in dedicated sessions, regularly updates on progress, and identifies concrete shared actions to make progress towards the goal. Goals do not need to remain forever. A three- or six-month timeframe for a goal is very motivating, and once the goal is reached or significant progress has been made, a new shared goal can be identified. Working towards these team goals is like strength training for the team, and a way to structure continuous improvement to the team. Research by psychologists Edwin Locke and Gary Latham shows that a well-crafted goal is a source of motivation and helps the team stay the course when they are faced with challenges and obstacles.

2.   **Clear Roles**

Team roles are not the same as the ubiquitous job descriptions. Job descriptions focus on the tasks, responsibilities, authorities, and reporting structure for each of the team members and are useful in most situations. A job description rarely refers to the connection with the other members of the team. It is the team roles that play a critical part in creating and strengthening the connections between the team members.

In addition to the technical or professional focus of the job descriptions, team roles are the non-technical contributions needed in a team. Teams need to make sure they stay on time, whether completing a meeting on time or delivering an output on schedule. The team may designate a timekeeper role to a team member who is comfortable with this kind of role. Another very different role could be the team's liaison: someone who regularly interacts with key stakeholders to keep them abreast of evolutions and to bring their ideas back to the team. Yet another role can be that of devil's advocate, someone who challenges the team to ensure all possible options have been thoroughly vetted before a decision is made. As Mary Shapiro explains in the *Harvard Business Review's* guide to leading teams, other possible team roles are the meeting facilitator, note taker, consensus builder, or rule keeper. The team can allocate these team roles based on the team members' preferences and perceived strengths.

Belbin® Team Roles is a powerful team assessment tool that supports the concept of team roles in a very rigorous way. Team members answer several questions about their preferences for certain types of behaviors or roles in different situations. Their team peers also assess how they perceive the preferences of each member of the team. Combining the self-assessment with the rating from the peers gives a balanced and powerful image of each team member within a team. Belbin® Team Roles recognizes nine different roles in a team. A few of them are "the shaper" who encourages and pushes the team to move forward, "the plant" who is good at bringing creative ideas and suggestion into the discussion, or "the team worker" who helps the team gel and ensures that the diversity in the team is used to its fullest potential. The Belbin® Team Roles report shows that each member of the team can fulfill these very different roles to a certain extent and in certain situations, but also points out what each member's "preferred" roles are. Each team member's profile is plotted on the team chart, showing their preferred roles and also which roles are really not a good fit. Members can clearly see which other members in the team are good at the roles they themselves prefer the least. This creates connections where each team member sees how others in the team compensate for the skills and strengths they are missing, and therefore on whom they can count for a particular type of role. A team session where the report is explored allows the team to identify its combined strengths, assign the nine team roles, and also highlight which roles are underrepresented on the team. In this way the roles distributed in the team are interdependent: those who have preferred roles take on roles on behalf of those who are not comfortable in them. This interdependency strengthens the connections and the sense of team, and demonstrates that every member contributes to the team through their preferred team roles.

3. **Team Norms**

Team norms are the principles the team formally identifies and agrees to adhere to, linked to decision-making, participation, engagement, or confidentiality. These norms are simple and should evolve. The team should create its own norms and regularly review the degree to which these are adhered to. Team norms should be referred to regularly and not just be dusted off when there are tensions or performance issues.

When a team needs to establish team norms for the first time, a simple activity can create an initial version of the team norms in a short time. Ask each team member to individually write down their best and worst team experiences and the reasons for their evaluations. This provides the key ingredients from which the team can discuss and extract common themes about what it wants to commit to in order to be successful and what it wants to avoid.

Examples of other teams' norms should not really serve as inspiration because norms are only meaningful and owned if the team creates them. Yet, a few examples can give an idea of the themes that team norms can cover.

An example of team norms for an anonymous team in Shapiro's guide:

As a team, we aspire to

Support each other fully: we will understand and appreciate others' lives, both at work and outside of work. We will create a climate where team members feel free to ask for help, offer help, and listen;

Communicate fully: we will share information and best practices, we will share what we do at work and in our lives, to better support one another, and we will share our successes to motivate ourselves and position our team to build upon those accomplishments;

Be innovative: we will develop a climate where it feels safe to take risks (including expressing ourselves) and experiment, and where downsides are identified but upsides are protected from naysaying.

When a company really values teamwork and wants to embed this in the culture, it can establish overall norms that the different teams operating at different divisions and levels adopt. As Ruth Wageman et al. share in their book *Senior Leadership Teams*, Applebee has established the following corporate team norms:

Build trust. Honesty and integrity, being loyal to and defending others—even when they aren't present—honoring commitments, no matter how small, keeping no secrets, respecting others, welcoming others' interest and questions about your area (no protecting of one's turf), collaborating, giving feedback, and developing others.

Be decisive. Taking measured risks, being innovative, admitting mistakes (recovering quickly and sharing your learnings), being courageous, and taking a stand on issues.

Be accountable. See it. Own it. Fix it.

Hold great meetings. Meetings should be well planned (with an agenda), start and end on time, and involve all attendees. Only one person should speak at a time. No sidebar conversations. Next steps and accountabilities should be summarized at the meeting's close.

Deliver results. Members should deliver on commitments by demonstrating "iron will determination to make it happen".

Demonstrate balance. Members should demonstrate and support work/life balance.

Have fun. Life is short.

Your team will for sure take a solid step forward once it has created and maintains a clear framework with a team goal, clear roles, and team norms. But a team is not a static unit that once formed remains unchanged. Changes will occur and they should be seen as part of the normal dynamics of a team, not as a setback. When a member leaves the team and needs to be replaced, or when a team needs to be expanded, the way a new member is recruited into the team can either strengthen the team or pull it apart.

RECRUITING FOR A TEAM

If you are convinced that you want to build your team into a high-performance team, and if you are well on the way to getting there, you also need to rethink how you recruit people into a team. In the usual way of recruiting, a couple of folks (most frequently a human resources representative and the recruit's future direct boss) will meet and evaluate the candidates. Based on the documents they receive, the candidate's references in some cases, and mostly the face-to-face exchanges with the candidates, they decide who the best fit is, using a combination of specific criteria and gut feeling. There can be multiple rounds to ultimately reduce the pool of candidates to the final selection. This is a time-consuming process both for the organization and the candidates. If at the end a candidate is hired, the others obviously feel disappointed and in some cases as having been assessed unfairly. The long and energy-consuming process is finally over, yet the foundations for lots of tensions and challenges have just been created.

This process signals to the rest of the organization that the person who ends up joining is really the best out there: of all the candidates only one survived and clearly fits all the requirements for the job, and then some. It is clear for the new recruits' peers that their direct boss and human resources department regard this person extremely well, and they have probably not found them to have many flaws. Although the direct boss expects that the new recruit's peers will be thrilled with this new high-caliber individual joining the team, the reality is often different. Since none of them were involved in the selection process, a natural skepticism creeps in, even for those with the most positive mindset. First impressions take only seven seconds, and when meeting a team member for the first time, many will be tempted to look for evidence not of their greatness but of something that the boss or human resources representative could have overlooked. This skepticism can exist long after the new member has joined the team, and despite all the get-to-know-one-another sessions that are organized. This is not an optimal start to building the connections between this new member and the team peers.

> " We focus on teamwork and
> avoid having star employees. "
> – Pablo Isla, CEO of Inditex and
> *Harvard Business Review* CEO of 2017

So what is a better way? How can we lay a better foundation for an integration and development of connections with the team members even before someone new joins the team, without adding more interview steps? In addition to involving team members, some approaches are more creative than the artificial setup of the job interview and use situations where multiple aspects and behaviors of the final candidates can be observed. I am sharing a few examples that I have seen used quite successfully.

TIP
Involve the team in recruiting their peers.

In an article in the WIAL global newsletter Helena Miyahara shares how a multinational company adapted the final steps of its recruitment process. The three or four final candidates are invited for a two-hour action learning session. They are put in a group with three of four members of their future team and receive some background information about a real challenge the company is facing. The human resources representative and direct boss sit outside of the group and observe. The action learning session is not a brainstorming session where participants compete to come up with the smartest solution. The ground rule of action learning is to use questions only to identify the root of a problem. The observers listen to how the shortlisted candidates contribute in the session. Are they trying to impose their ideas under the guise of leading questions? Or are they asking powerful questions that open up new ways of looking at the problem? Do they tend to show how much they know, or do they show an interest to learn from others? And how does each of the candidates connect with the other members in the session? Do they build on others' ideas or do they just stay with their own train of thought? This kind of session allows the organization to see the candidates in real interaction with some of their future colleagues. It is possible to fake an interview, but it is much more difficult to fake a session where you interact with others. This session gives the human resources representative and direct boss a live observation of how the candidates work with others, and the existing team members share their observations on each of the candidates after the session. The candidates themselves, even those who end up not being selected, feel taken seriously when they can contribute to finding solutions for a challenge the organization is facing. They also feel that they get a better understanding of the company culture through the exchange with those who currently work for it.

Robert Kegan and Lisa Lahey reveal that during recruitment drives at Next Jump, a large number of candidates spend an entire day in a series of exercises and exchanges with current members of the organization. An in-house app allows for real-time and constant evaluation of the different candidates by the current team members. Next Jump has a very particular view of the company culture they want to maintain, and the assessments focus only on how candidates match with that culture, not on their knowledge or experience. One criterion they look out for is how humble the candidates are, or how they can deal with setbacks when facing challenges. The ratings compiled by the Next Jump team members about all the candidates they interacted with that day give a pretty good aggregate view of how each candidate aligns with the company culture.

The advantages of getting your team members involved in the final selection of their new team peers are numerous compared to having only the human resources representative and direct boss make the decision: most significant of these advantages are a deeper level of team engagement with the new team member and a stronger commitment to make this member succeed in the team. Who would want their recommended hire to fail?

CONCLUSION

If you are convinced that building a high-performance team is what you want your leadership to be about, it's important to make sure the basics are in place and function well. Too often we get excited by the latest idea and jump on that thinking it will make the difference, before putting the basics into practice. The basics are called that for a reason: a team cannot function without them. So make sure the following basic elements are in place, and remain in place:

- Don't wait for tensions to start working on your team: whenever "now" is, start now
- The ideal number of members in a team is six or seven; do not ask who else could be added but assess if everyone is really critical to the team mission
- Get the basics—key indicators, one-on-one meetings, and a regular team meeting—in place, and keep them in place
- Foster learning within the team and amongst team members as a way to share knowledge and experience and strengthen the team dynamics

- When ready, develop with the team members team goals, clear roles, and team norms, and follow up on these all the time
- When it comes to recruiting a new member to a team, make the recruitment process a team task

GROWING YOUR TEAM

THE KEY TO HIGH-PERFORMANCE TEAMS

When you google "high-performance teams" you will find a wealth of resources claiming to reveal the ultimate secret about high-performance teams. Experts claim that their model, framework, or insight holds the key to unlocking your team's potential. Some say that the only thing that really counts is a clear vision, others say it's trust, others still say it's all about communication, or respect, or diversity, or having a real great team leader. When Google itself wanted to find out why some of its own teams were more effective than others, they didn't turn to experts or consultants, but analyzed in detail data about their own teams. Project Aristotle, led by Google analyst Julia

Rozovsky, took two years and studied 180 different teams. The project collected both quantitative data like team composition or performance as well as qualitative feedback from interviews, and looked for patterns in all these data, trying to find out why for some teams Aristotle's "the whole is larger than the sum of its parts" really held true, while for other teams the extreme opposite happened. In Charles Duhiggs' article on Google's quest to build the perfect team, Abeer Dubey, a manager in Google's People Analytics division, shared that one of the first conclusions that the researchers made was contrary to what they had expected:

> We had lots of data, but there was nothing showing that a mix of specific personality types or skills or backgrounds made any difference. The "who" part of the equation didn't seem to matter. Team norms are what makes the difference.

Characteristics often identified as the critical factors to high-performance teams, such as diversity, shared goals, or individual performance did not show a solid correlation with team performance. In other words, and as an example, some teams with a high level of diversity were working as high-performance teams but some were not. And some teams with very limited diversity were high-performance teams, while others were not. When the researchers looked further into how team norms (most often unwritten) differed across teams, they came across a concept that aligned very well with their observations: team psychological safety! They found that team psychological safety is the biggest factor impacting team performance and is four times more significant than the other factors they identified (dependability, structure and clarity, meaning, and impact). In Google's study, teams with a high level of team psychological safety had two traits that did not appear in other teams: "equality in distribution of conversational turn-taking" and "high average social sensitivity". Equality in distribution of conversational turn-taking means that on average, team members speak the same amount of time, as opposed to teams where a few members are doing all the talking while others can't get their ideas shared or are unwilling or uncomfortable to share them. High average social sensitivity indicates that team members are aware of how others feel based on their tone of voice, their expressions, and other nonverbal cues. They seem to know when someone disagrees or feels uncomfortable and take that into account when moving the team forward. In average or low performance teams, team members are less aware of others' feelings or emotions, or ignore them. The real difference between high-performance teams and the rest is not about who is on the team, but how the team members interact. When Google shared these results on its open platform, many reacted as if the holy grail of high-performance teams had finally been uncovered!

TEAM PSYCHOLOGICAL SAFETY

The concept of team psychological safety had in fact been developed and validated by Professor Amy Edmondson from Harvard University more than 20 years earlier, but remained mostly a topic of study in academic circles. In her article "Psychological Safety and Learning Behavior in Work Teams", she describes team psychological safety as a "shared belief by members of a team that the team is safe for interpersonal risk-taking".

We are all familiar with risk-taking, in particular with taking a financial risk. Taking a risk means doing something and not knowing for sure what the outcome will be. Of course, we hope for a positive outcome; when taking a financial risk, the financial gain is the reason behind taking the risk. But we know that the outcome is not guaranteed, and that we might also have a negative outcome where we lose money. If the outcome is guaranteed, it is not a risk. Putting money in a fixed interest deposit account is not taking a risk. If I take a financial risk and the outcome is positive (a gain), I will most likely repeat this kind of risk-taking or try to replicate and repeat my thinking or strategy. If the first risk pays off, I am inclined to repeat the risk-taking based on my success. If, however the outcome of my risk-taking is negative, I will probably review my strategy. I might once again try the same risk, but if my second attempt turns out bad again, I will most likely not continue to take my financial risks in the same way because I seem to continue to lose money.

Edmondson applies the notion of risk-taking to the interpersonal dimension, and the same reasoning as with financial risks applies. Taking a risk in my interactions with others means I am not sure of the outcome ahead of time. The outcome is how the others will react—what they will say and do after I have taken my interpersonal risk. I hope for a positive outcome, but since this is a risk, I know there might be a negative outcome. Examples of interpersonal risks are asking for, giving, or rejecting help or advice, speaking up about an issue, defending unpopular positions, admitting you don't know or don't understand, or sharing personal and private feelings or experiences. When taking any of these risks with others, I hope they will appreciate my question or comment, or explain what is not clear for me; in general, I hope they will consider the risk I took beneficial for them or the team. But I am aware that the outcome may not always be this positive. Some team members may ridicule me (face-to-face or, more likely, behind my back) or accuse me of having a negative mindset. If I take interpersonal risks, and the outcome is positive, I will be inclined to take these risks again because the outcome (the gain) encourages me. If the outcome is negative, however, I may at most give it another try, but if I am faced with the same negative outcome again, I will quickly stop taking this kind of interpersonal risk. The social context in work environments, whether it is in one-on-one or in team settings, is often threatening rather than motivating. When team members are concerned others will ridicule them, directly or behind their backs, or when they fear that what they say will be held against them at some point in the future, they will remain quiet. This means that problems remain hidden, misunderstandings linger, and work is suboptimal. Although managers and organizations in general will say that they want team members to speak up, the reality is that, as Edmondson puts it, "nobody was ever fired for keeping silent", while the other way around maybe happens more often.

Edmondson's research found that team psychological safety has a direct impact on the way a team learns. If team members feel they can safely express their doubts, questions, or concerns, the team will quickly identify problems and find ways to solve them rather than discover gaps or misunderstandings weeks or months later. The team will be in a continuous learning cycle, asking, "What are we doing that works well? What is not working well? What should we change?" Team learning supports the team and builds up better performance over time.

In the original team psychological safety studies, Edmondson looked at how surgical teams adopt new cardiac procedures. Some teams were very hierarchical, with the main surgeon the head of the team and nurses, assistants, and operating theatre personnel executing the surgeon's instructions. Although this was a team where everybody had a key and distinct role to play (each had clear descriptions), lower ranked members were uncomfortable speaking up when they saw an issue or had a concern about the way the procedure was going. They preferred pretending all was fine and hoping for the best. The head surgeon didn't really ask the others on the team for their thoughts or input. Nobody on the team was taking any interpersonal risks and they felt that remaining quiet was their safest option. Teams with low psychological safety actually reported fewer errors when using the new cardiac procedure. It turned out that in fact they did make errors but the climate in the team prevented anyone from speaking up and reporting them, so the mistakes were not identified, did not get addressed, and were repeated. The team was slower to learn the new procedure, and its performance (the number of successful surgeries) built up slowly over the weeks. Other surgical teams worked very differently. In teams with higher psychological safety, every member of the team, including the lowest ranking in terms of the team's structure, was comfortable speaking up when they thought something was not okay, and their comments or questions were accepted as a way to make progress. The head surgeon was comfortable with sharing his uncertainties when he had any or asking other members of the team for their ideas. These teams actually reported more errors because they did not hesitate to speak up about abnormal situations. Once an error was reported, it got addressed and did not reoccur. As a result, the team learned faster and their success rate and performance in using the new procedure rose faster. Team psychological safety is not some generic concept that is good to have in the team; it is a key to the way the team learns more rapidly. Learning more effectively is how a team's performance increases.

Google's internal research on high-performance teams found that the level of psychological safety in the team is by far the most determining factor of the team's performance. Psychological safety is the degree to which team members are comfortable with taking risks with the others in the team: asking for help, speaking up when disagreeing, or giving honest feedback. Teams that can develop this dynamic are most likely to do well both in terms of team engagement and motivation (the "soft" part) and team performance (the "hard" part). Although the team leader plays a very important role in building the climate and in leading by example, the leader is not who determines the level of psychological safety in the team. Psychological safety is a real team concept and depends on what happens within the different connections in the team. "It's not about the leader, it's about the team!" is how the managing director of an outsourcing firm succinctly put it!

IT'S HOW WE ARE WIRED

When Professor Amy Edmondson first developed the concept of team psychological safety more than 20 years ago, neuroscience was starting to gain ground. Today, we have solid evidence that team psychological safety is not just an idea or a theoretical concept but actually corresponds with how the human brain works.

Our human brain has developed tremendously since our forefathers walked the earth. When they were facing physical threats like an aggressive predator approaching their living quarters or a violent thunder and lightning storm, they quickly learned that it is better to hide or run away. Those who thought it was a good idea to attack the predator didn't survive and their genes weren't passed on to future generations. Humans came to develop instincts that allowed them to quickly decide what was a threat—and run away—or what was a safe situation they could approach. Our brains developed shortcuts to make these decisions, so they became instantaneous. When faced with an obvious threat to our lives, we do not need to sit down to weigh the pros and cons: our brain makes an immediate decision that allows us to act quickly so we can survive. Although most of us are no longer dealing with wild predators in our daily lives, our brain deals in the same way with the modern-day physical threats that surround us. When faced with a threat like a car speeding towards us, our brain will prioritize survival and use all its focus and energy to deal with the threat quickly and effectively.

Neuroscience shows that the same patterns of brain activity occur when we are facing not physical or life-threatening threats, but social threats; the same brain circuitry we have developed to protect us from physical threats is activated when we are facing social threats. When the colleague whom we cannot stand walks into the office, our brain activity is similar to when we are facing a physical threat. The team leader who embarrassed you in front of everybody in the last team meeting would engage the same brain activity as if he were about to physically attack you.

When our brain is focusing on social (not physical) survival, all its physiological energy is dedicated to that survival. The parts of the brain taking care of survival are in overdrive and the other parts of the brain that deal with problem solving, coming up with new ideas, thinking, or processing information are left without energy. Edmondson summarizes it in a simple yet powerful way in her book *The Fearless Organization*: "It's hard for people to do their best when they are afraid".

Director of the NeuroLeadership Institute Dr. David Rock asserts that the opposite of social threats are social rewards. These are situations where we feel good and safe, where the social environment is encouraging and supportive, and we feel appreciated by those with whom we interact. Social threats put our brain in survival mode and social rewards bring a sense of safety and belonging, which allows our full and creative participation and contribution within the social group. Our brain can focus all its energy on learning, sharing, brainstorming, or being an effective member of the team. It is not just a matter of "balancing out" social threats with a few social rewards. Building psychological safety in a team requires lots of social rewards and can be easily destroyed by just a single socially threatening situation. In his book *The Culture Code*, Daniel Coyle emphasizes this sense of belonging:

> A mere hint of belonging is not enough; one or two signals are not enough. We are built to require lots of signaling, over and over. This is why a sense of belonging is easy to destroy and hard to build.

Social psychology professor Matthew Lieberman notes that humans are social animals and how we interact with others strongly impacts our wellbeing. Our forefathers ensured that they were needed by their tribe and therefore would not be excluded. Being expelled by the tribe was equivalent to a death sentence. In our modern society, the tribe is replaced by work colleagues. Britt Andreatta summarizes well what a sense of purpose and meaning in a work situation comes down to: "At work, what matters for most people is feeling they can make a contribution and that others value their work." This amounts to being valued by the work group and knowing there is a safe place where they belong. From a tribal perspective, it means they are needed by the group and therefore less likely to be ousted. Neurologically, that sense of security is enough to settle the amygdala and allow people to reach higher-order thinking skills like logical analysis and innovation.

Team psychological safety is not a monolithic "thing" that either exists or does not exist. Edmondson's research confirmed that the belief that the team is a safe place for interpersonal risk-taking is actually built up of several elements. Each of the following elements can be assessed and developed to strengthen the team's overall level of psychological safety.

MUTUAL SUPPORT

When asked, most professionals would say that they of course support others because they are aware it's the right thing to do! Social psychologists David Johnson and Roger Johnson's research on hundreds of work groups concluded that cooperative work groups are much more successful than work groups in which members compete with one another. In reality though, the *Harvard Business Review* article "Why Strategy Execution Unravels and What to Do About It" reveals that 84% of managers say they can rely on their boss and their direct reports all or most of the time, while only 9% say they can rely on peers in other functions and units all the time and 50% say they can rely on them most of the time. When managers feel they cannot rely on colleagues in other functions or units, they compensate with dysfunctional behaviors that sub-optimize execution and ultimately lead to conflicts.

Supporting others as a general idea works well as long as business as usual prevails. The depth and intensity of the mutual support reveals itself when the team is facing a complex challenge or even a crisis, or a situation where one team member's priorities adversely impact others' priorities. If these challenges can be discussed, all members can stay connected as a team, and when an optimal solution can be found, the team will progress. That's why Reg Revans calls the members of an action learning problem-solving group "comrades in adversity". A team will become stronger if it smartly deals with and overcomes the challenge. If, however, the sense of being comrades is damaged, if personal priorities take precedence and members focus on their own priorities to the detriment of those of others in the team, a negative atmosphere starts to build. The sense of team quickly dissipates when team members see that not all are pulling in the same direction or that some members' actions are undermining the efforts of others. Team members prioritize their own direct responsibilities, team efforts become disconnected, and the team avoids dealing with the real issues—until these appear again and start to adversely impact the team performance.

When a team faces an emergency, there is little time to create good habits. Explicitly making giving and receiving support a normal and regular way of working—as opposed to waiting for a crisis—strengthens the team and prepares it to better deal with challenging situations. Putting explicit effort in developing mutual support is a key requirement for a team to reach genuine collaboration as opposed to just coordination. Simple routines, such as each team member regularly taking the time to share the top three priorities in their area of responsibility, help build awareness of what is going on for each member of the team. Knowing what others are dealing with and focusing on opens up possibilities to offer support and create connections. These exchanges need to be kept fluid and should not become too formal. For many years, knowledge management advocates promoted the creation of knowledge repositories to ensure all that is known is captured, but in reality, these significant efforts rarely bring tangible improvements in collaboration. More recent efforts have tried to make knowledge available in a more fluid and punctual way, hoping that participants will explore available knowledge when they need it, and trying to build frequent engagement through the use of more human media. With video quickly becoming the premium medium of information sharing (video content is expected to represent 75% of world's mobile data traffic by 2020), new solutions for knowledge sharing are centered on the organization's members themselves. A Canadian company created a tool called HELPFUL where members of an organization load up very short videos in which they share what they are working on. Quick and easy to digest, these videos create awareness of the multiple initiatives that are going on in the organization and incite members to offer support or ask for help more fluidly.

One technique I have frequently used with new teams, and even more with established teams, is the Needs and Offers process. It is a powerful activity where great progress can be made in just half a day. In my experience with teams, this activity always leads to powerful insights and puts the spotlight on the fact that so much potential remains untapped. The Needs and Offers session leads to meaningful discussions where team members who have been working alongside one another (as opposed to with one another) discover for the first time what challenges others experience in their areas of responsibility, and creates awareness that all are better off if they can receive and offer support. Find out exactly how the Needs and Offers activity works in the Team Technique #1 highlight.

TEAM TECHNIQUE #1: NEEDS AND OFFERS

Each team member takes some time to write down what they need from each of the others in the team to be successful in their own specific area of responsibility. The requests (needs) must be very specific: "I need a reply to my emails within 48 hours" is clear and can be evaluated, whereas "I need full cooperation from you" is very much open to interpretation. In the next step, each member of the team collects all the requests the other team members have made of them. Each studies the requirements, asks any clarifying questions if needed (no debate or discussion), and replies to each of the needs by making an offer under the form of A, B, C, or D. An A offer stands for "absolute support", meaning the member will commit to fully comply with this need. A B offer means "bounded support", meaning the need will be fulfilled for a certain period of time or for a specific type, for example "reply to requests within 48 hours for existing clients" for a need expressed as "reply to requests within 48 hours". C stands for "conditional support", meaning the team member will satisfy the need if another condition is met, for example "reply to the email if there is a clear question or call for action in the message". Finally, D signifies "decline", meaning this need cannot be fulfilled. Once all team members have prepared their offers, the final step in the process is for pairs of team members to sit down together and review their needs and offers, to clarify where needed, and to negotiate so that optimal solutions are found for all team members pairs, and for the team as a whole.

ASKING FOR HELP

Asking for help seems so simple and we do it all the time in a variety of circumstances. But in the work environment, asking for help is often seen as a risky endeavor. In an environment where we are assessed on the expertise we possess or the competencies and decisiveness we exhibit, asking for help makes many uncomfortable because it seems to diminish their status or points to a lack of autonomy. Yet as psychologist Heidi Grant describes in her research around the challenges people have asking for help, it is simply impossible not to develop collaboration with others inside and outside your team or organization:

> It's virtually impossible to advance in modern organizations without assistance from others. Cross-functional teams, agile project management techniques, matrixed or hierarchy-minimizing structures, and increasingly collaborative office cultures require you to constantly push for the cooperation and support of your managers, peers, and employees. Your performance, development, and career progression depend more than ever on your seeking out the advice, referrals, and resources you need.

Another discomfort when it comes to asking for help is that we are afraid of rejection and overestimate the probability of getting a negative reply. The reality is actually very different: people are more willing to help than we estimate. In Heidi Grant's research experiments, compliance was 48% higher than help seekers expected, and people put more effort in helping others than we think. Wharton Professor Adam Grant confirmed that the opportunity to help others is for many a factor of motivation in the workplace. It was Maslow who first suggested that we are motivated to do things that are personally meaningful for us; Adam Grant's insight was that for most people in most lines of work, doing something meaningful means helping others. As social psychology professor Matthew Lieberman explained, it's hard to find meaning in what we do if at some level it doesn't help someone else or makes someone happier.

The following anecdote attributed to Steve Jobs illustrates that asking for help should really be something simple that we are not scared of:

> I have never found anybody that didn't want to help me if I asked them for help. I called up Bill Hewlett when I was 12 years old. "Hi, I'm Steve Jobs. I'm 12 years old. I'm a student in high school. I want to build a frequency counter and I was wondering if you have any spare parts I could have." He laughed and gave me the spare parts, and he gave me a job that summer at Hewlett-Packard.
>
> I have never found anyone who said no or hung up the phone when I called. I just asked. And when people ask me, I try to be responsive, to pay that debt of gratitude back. Most people never pick up the phone and call. Most people never ask, and that's what separates, sometimes, the people who do things from the people who just dream about them.

A team cannot become a high-performance team if the members are afraid of asking for help. Making asking for help a recurring practice will allow the team to develop meaningful connections amongst themselves and build up the comfort and confidence to ask for help outside of the team as well. Detailed in the Team Technique #2 highlight, the HELP! Board is a simple technique that a team can put in place and keep in place for the entire period that they are working together. Asking for help is really the key to exploring and exploiting the resources, talents, and competencies within the team as well as in its environment. A team that can develop this practice is poised for better learning and better performance.

TEAM TECHNIQUE #2: HELP! BOARD

The team makes asking for help as ubiquitous as getting a cup of coffee by setting up a HELP! Board in a central location where all team members can easily and regularly see it. It can be also posted as a shared document for a virtual team. Two types of pre-printed Post-It®-style tags are available near the HELP! Board. One is the "I NEED HELP" tag where team members who need help can write their names and the topic or area where help is needed. The second type is the "I CAN HELP" tag where another team member can offer help, specifying exactly which part of the need he or she can satisfy. The board should at all times look like a work in progress. This is an internal tool for the team and it is not necessary to make it too formal.

Writing up these tags and displaying them for all to see may seem more cumbersome than just going and asking for help, but it visually creates and emphasizes a supportive dynamic within the team by making everyone see how normal it is to ask others for help. Once in a while, the "I NEED HELP" tags that remain unanswered are brought into a team discussion to see how these needs can be addressed by the team as a whole.

DEALING WITH TOUGH AND COMPLEX PROBLEMS

In leadership development, self-awareness is what makes the difference between average and great leaders. It is difficult to develop and progress if one does not know one's strengths, weaknesses, and what to focus on. In a team setting, this is equivalent to a shared awareness about the team's strengths and areas for improvement. Very often, team members are very aware of what is not working well, but how the team deals with the issues can differ widely. Does the team find a way to constructively look for improvements, or do they avoid dealing with the elephant in the room? A high-performance team is able to bring up team process and performance issues and look for solutions themselves. When team members can openly discuss what is not working well and explore possible solutions, they enter into a cycle of continuous learning. When issues are avoided or not discussed openly for fear of upsetting the status quo or creating tensions or conflict with others—or when issues end up on the team leader's desk waiting for a decision—the team gets stuck and collaboration and performance issues persist and limit the team's progress. Everybody may seem superficially happy when keeping the peace is the priority, but by avoiding problems, the issues holding the team back will keep growing larger and larger. Fear of bringing up taboo issues because it may cause conflict means these are not dealt with, and this leads to an impact far bigger than the avoided conflict would have made. Organizational psychologist Roger Schwartz tells us that people often overstate the risk of bringing up an issue and underestimate the benefit of bringing it up and dealing with it.

Dealing with uncomfortable issues is by definition a challenge, and bringing them up is taking an obvious interpersonal risk. It takes time and practice for a team to develop this habit. One way to start is to create and maintain the habit of sharing feedback, about both task-related and people-related issues. Although this will for sure be uncomfortable at first, the discomfort is normal and necessary for the team to grow. As Patrick Lencioni shares, avoiding holding team members accountable for their contributions and impact on the team is one of the key challenges teams face. Regularly scheduled check-ins about task and people issues remind team members that it is only by raising the issues and dealing with them that the team will develop. Here again, it is better to start developing this habit now, when there are no obvious tensions or conflicts.

It may be worthwhile to start off with anonymity. You can ask team members to write down what kind of behavior or habits are holding the team back. All the issues are put into a bowl and each is picked and read out randomly by a different member of the team. The team has a discussion about how to deal with the issue and commit to taking initial steps to improve the situation, keeping the focus on the issue, not on the messenger. The issues should be treated as challenges for the team, not an issue related to a particular team member.

Diversity of thought can lead to improved performance if the focus is on discussing and opposing the ideas, not the persons behind the ideas. Schwartz identifies as one of the eight behaviors of smarter teams the focus on "reasoning and intent" when dealing with difficult issues. Rather than defending positions or solutions, focusing on interests and needs allows others to ask questions and share how their views are different from yours. Discussing needs allows the team to build solutions that favorably answer the different needs. Discussing only positions or solutions at best leads to sub-optimal compromises, and at worst to discontent and stalemate. Teams that avoid bringing up difficult issues may avoid conflict, but not dealing with them brings significant negative impact in the long run.

In addition to building the capability to deal with tough and sensitive issues, you should also consider what your team is actually working on. When we think of top management and the C-suite, we assume they spend their time together elaborating strategy, making long-term business decisions, and crafting the organization's future. The reality is that leadership teams, surprisingly and counter-intuitively, are inclined to spend most of their time on trivial things. This phenomenon was identified by historian and author C. Northcote Parkinson when he found that a leadership team spent much more time discussing the design, features, and color of a bike shed that needed to be built and that would cost a couple of thousand dollars, than on a strategic investment in a new plant which represented millions of dollars. Termed the bike-shed effect or Parkinson's law of triviality, it is a tendency of teams to give a disproportionate amount of attention to trivial issues and details. People— at all levels, not just top teams—are inclined to spend an inordinate amount of time on details. When discussing in which colors the new product should be made available to the market, pretty much everyone has an idea or can express an opinion, and this leads to never-ending discussions and debates. When the discussion is about how new technologies will impact the company in five years, or how the company's strategy should be modified to deal with an unpredictable environment, leaders often refrain from taking a stance because the topic is complex, vague, and uncertain, and their opinions are more consequential and more open to criticism than in the case of issues with lower importance.

What is your team spending its time on? A team should be more than just the aggregation or coordination of each team member's priorities. In fact, a team should stay clear of anything that can be handled by individual members, business units, or functions, not only to use the team's time wisely but to build a real sense of team and purpose. The team's real "raison d'être" is dealing with major and business-critical tasks that need to be worked on and owned by the entire team. Identifying what the team priorities are creates the real sense and value of being a team.

Too often teams think of meetings when they reflect on how they spend their time together. The team meetings become reporting sessions where each takes turn giving updates, with others chipping in (or not). Nothing is being created here and very little teamwork is taking place. It takes courage and some team discipline to stick to the agreed priorities because there is always a multitude of trivial or even frivolous issues that clamor for attention or a decision, and that end up using valuable time. You cannot let the team's agenda be determined by whatever hot new issue pops up each day in some corner of the organization. The simple to-do list helps individuals keep track of priorities; creating a Team To-Do List makes as much sense. Moreover, spending some time as a team to discuss and agree on what to spend its shared time on is in itself a valuable team routine! For details on how to take advantage of a Team To-Do List, see the Team Technique #3 highlight.

TEAM TECHNIQUE #3: TEAM TO-DO LIST

A team should establish criteria about what it will work on as a team and the process by which new topics are added to its agenda. Without a priority list that is shared with and constantly visible to everyone in the team (and to those outside of the team), precious time will be sucked up by petty details. The power of the to-do list lies not in that it gets work done, but that it provides focus and reminders.

1	**2**
MANAGE	**FOCUS**
Crises and Pressing Problems	On Strategies and Values
Demand and necessity Daily fire-fighting Be quick to delegate	Opportunity and planning Keep critical thinking Consider the macro
IMPORTANT AND URGENT	**IMPORTANT NOT URGENT**
3	**4**
AVOID	**LIMIT**
Interruptions and Busy Work	The Trivial and Wasteful
Illusion and deception Not your emergency Minimize investment	Escape and waste Entertainment only Use to minimize waste
NOT IMPORTANT AND NOT URGENT	**URGENT NOT IMPORTANT**

The Eisenhower matrix is a popular time management tool for prioritizing and monitoring tasks, applicable both at the level of the individual and the level of the team. For the team, it provides a simple canvas on which to discuss what is important versus not so important and what is urgent versus not urgent. Each quarter, team members can individually propose or collectively brainstorm potential topics, and then have a discussion about which quadrant on the Eisenhower matrix these topics belong in. The majority of the team's priorities should be in the "focus" area. Spending a few hours each quarter to update the to-do list, evaluate progress, and get alignment for the following months, builds team cohesion and provides focus.

Once the list of non-urgent and important team priorities is clear and agreed upon, it is critical that these are worked on by the whole team, not divided into smaller portions and delegated to sub-teams or individuals. This is especially important for senior leadership teams working on the organization's strategic priorities, as pointed out by Ruth Wageman et al.:

Keep the task large. One of the most common reasons leadership teams focus on the small issues is that leaders and members tend to disaggregate the big tasks into small pieces and distribute these amongst the team members. The understanding is that individual pieces will be sewn back together. It can feel this makes the work more manageable. But it sidesteps what should be the real work of the team: making the big decisions interdependently. Avoid this kind of piecework. Keep the core team small and the large tasks large.

Having each team member work on a part of the problem, then reconvene and "agree" on how to move forward is coordination at best but for sure not collaboration, agrees Britt Andreatta. Collaboration can only happen when all team members are sitting around the table (or in a virtual session), exchanging ideas, defending positions, building alternatives, co-creating optimum solutions, and collectively owning the output of the working session. A team is only performing when work gets done.

What would this look like? Let's say an important challenge arises, where there are conflicting opinions and the team needs to find a way forward. The leader can invite the team to take ownership of the challenge and develop a solution. The team works and learns together when trying to move forward. Using the available input (customer feedback, stakeholder input, company objectives, or areas for improvement), the team creates, tests, brainstorms, and tries things out. They learn what works and what doesn't work, and from this shared experience, build together anything from a one-month action plan to a two-year roadmap. The focus of the team's work is not only on finding solutions to the problem, but also on the team's development by ensuring all voices are heard, all viewpoints are explored, and special attention is given to minority opinions, as Steven Beebe and John Masterson explain in their book on group communication. The level of team ownership—and therefore commitment—that the team has towards the solution it co-created is very different from what the team feels when finding out during the team leader's yearly "here's our plan" meeting what the road ahead looks like!

REACTING TO MISTAKES

You might be familiar with the story of Tom Watson Jr., CEO of IBM, who was faced with a young executive who had made bad decisions that cost the company several million dollars. When called to the CEO's office, the young man expected to be fired, but instead Watson said, "Not at all, after all we just spent a couple of million dollars educating you." Learning from our mistakes is universally accepted wisdom and Albert Einstein encouraged innovation by saying, "Anyone who has never made a mistake never tried anything new." However, the reality seems quite different in the workplace. In the team psychological safety measurements I have completed with several teams, the way the team reacts to mistakes was consistently rated as the most problematic. Most team members therefore find that speaking up about mistakes is the most challenging of interpersonal risks in a team.

Making mistakes is a key component of learning and improving. Mistakes big and small happen at all levels. It is how the team reacts to a mistake that impacts how it progresses from the situation. If a team can freely discuss the different mistakes that happen, and turn these into learning opportunities, a strong foundation for improvement develops. A high-performance team will look at a mistake as something the whole team is accountable for, even if it was a particular team member who made the mistake. When comparing why some cognitively diverse teams performed much better than others, UK researchers Alison Reynolds and David Lewis found that high-performance teams treated mistakes with curiosity, and they shared responsibility for getting the mistake fixed.

If mistakes are personalized and become the butt of jokes or gossip, team members will tend to hide them. This impacts performance and creates a culture of opaqueness rather than openness. Team members will cover up mistakes, build up facades with those around them, and push the blame on others when challenged. If team members think others are responsible for the mistakes, accountability drops and taking the necessary actions to deal with the situation is avoided. For some time, all may seem well since issues are swept under the carpet and confrontations are avoided. But in the long run, hidden mistakes will backfire and impact performance.

> Create a culture where it is okay
> to make mistakes but unacceptable
> not to learn from them.
> – Ray Dalio, billionaire hedge fund manager
> and philanthropist

Most mistakes are not of the million-dollar kind and it would be unwise to consider that the bigger the mistake the more opportunity for learning there is. The real learning is in the small mistakes that occur on a regular basis and the way the team creates a habit of talking about and learning from them. In *Teaming*, Professor Amy Edmondson writes that employees have two options when dealing with small mistakes in daily work. They can try to address the underlying issue, but this requires them to take interpersonal risks by opening up about the mistake to others, exposing their own or others' poor performance. Or they can compensate for the issue with rework, thus making the mistake go unnoticed. This means there is no learning from the occurrence. Rework and workarounds build up over time and become a burden of inefficiency that remains unaddressed. Failure is only debilitating if the lessons learned are not disseminated and applied. Small failures should be seen as early warning signs that are vital to avoid catastrophic failure in the future, and in the same vein, acknowledging small performance gaps is key to learning and avoiding larger failures down the road.

There are a number of approaches to make talking about mistakes as commonplace as talking about performance results or client feedback. One way is to focus on looking ahead, building reflection on improvement possibilities into the different work routines. Asking what went well, what could be better, and what could be done differently next time builds the habit of constantly looking for ways to do things better next time, without necessarily calling out any mistakes. This is more future-oriented and learning-based than the root cause analysis that is often used to drill down into why errors happened (such as Toyota's Five Why approach where the root cause of a problem is determined by repeating the question "Why?" five times and each answer forms the basis of the next question).

Some companies go much further and address mistakes head-on. The 50 Shades of Mistakes technique, explained in the Team Technique #4 highlight, purposely creates a topic of discussion and learning around mistakes even when no major mistakes occur. This technique and other similar ones build up the belief that mistakes are a way to learn and progress, and that a team should cultivate mistakes as the fertilizer to grow: finding and reporting mistakes becomes a key responsibility of each team member. Robert Kegan and Lisa Lahey share in their book that some organizations log problems and failures into a database, and team members record their own contribution and the contribution of others to the mistakes that were made. Entering data into the log is considered a great contribution to helping the organization learn. Not recording a mistake is considered a serious professional misstep that has consequences. In an article for the *Harvard Business Review*, Scott Anthony et al. writes that Spotify uses a whiteboard "fail wall" where all small and large issues that went wrong during a project are posted and that serves as the starting point for the project post mortem.

TEAM TECHNIQUE #4: 50 SHADES OF MISTAKES

Not all mistakes are created equal. Edmondson created a spectrum along which to rate mistakes. On one side of the spectrum are the "blameworthy" mistakes, that can be attributed to deviance or lack of attention. This kind of mistakes should not be celebrated. Yet too often, mistakes are lobbed in this category and the first question is "Who did it?" On the other side of the spectrum are the praiseworthy mistakes, those that pinpoint an issue in the process or human capability, or that happened because of changing and unfamiliar circumstances. These mistakes should be applauded because they allow the team to correct the process, address the capability gap, or evaluate the options. When asking a team to have a discussion about where mistakes belong, the spectrum makes it clear that very few mistakes belong in the blameworthy category.

One team that struggled with dealing with mistakes decided that in their Monday morning meeting, each team member would share one mistake they had made in the previous week. The team leader led by example by always having a mistake ready to share. The team would discuss each mistake, record it based on the team consensus along the spectrum scale, and each time identify one main learning. The first sessions were a bit awkward, but this became a powerful practice and talking about mistakes became much less of a challenge than in the past. Mistakes and the resulting learning became part of the team's vocabulary. Opening up about small mistakes, with very little consequences, prepared the team to deal with more important mistakes in a professional and positive way.

As Edmondson writes in *Teaming*, there is no such thing as a universal evaluation of mistakes, and mistakes need to be looked at in the context in which a particular team operates. In operations such as manufacturing or high-risk sensitive environments, mistakes need to be avoided at all cost. This is done through standardization, preventive inspection, automation, and the elimination of uncertainty. A team in this context needs to "organize to execute" and the focus is on repeating the same processes over and over again faultlessly. In more complex operations or operations that require creative exploration, the degree of uncertainty is much higher, and mistakes are a way for the team to learn and innovate. Here, teams need to "organize to learn".

PRACTICE, PRACTICE, PRACTICE

When thinking about high-performance teams, the images that most often come to mind or pop up in an online search are those of sports teams or music bands. These teams, in order to perform at their peak, spend most of their time practicing. When we admire them playing their sport or performing their music, we see the team in action at most for a couple of hours. Yet, countless hours, weeks, and months of rehearsing, trying things out, and practicing precede that performance. This practice is what allows the team to perform and deliver. It is accepted that practice need not be perfect. It is exactly the purpose of practice to try, adjust, and redo until the overall performance is at its best. As Kegan and Lahey emphasize, when practicing, there is no result or performance at stake:

> When we're practicing, we are not expecting (and others are not expecting us) to perform perfectly. In naming what we're doing "practice", we signal that we're experimenting, trying something on, working at improving. And we clarify that practice

is what we're supposed to be doing—trying hard to get better at it. We're creating conditions in which we won't feel pressure to demonstrate expertise, conditions that will allow us to experiment, that will allow us to gather feedback, that will help us learn.

Any team needs practice: for sure, no team will get things right the first time. But how do we practice running a meeting, doing a project, negotiating with a client, or launching a new product? How does a team in an organization practice so it can become a high-performance team? Psychologist Mihaly Csikszentmihalyi coined the concept of "flow" when an athlete at the height of his skill reaches a state of enjoyment when training or performing despite the physical effort and strain. Yet when that practice stops, the enjoyment quickly disappears:

> An athlete who does not run regularly will soon be out of shape and will no longer enjoy running. Any manager knows that his company will start falling apart if his attention wanders. In each case, without concentration, a complex activity breaks down into chaos.

In her article "Psychological Safety, Trust, and Learning: A Group-Level Lens", Edmondson says that practice fields are "opportunities for teams to practice and to reflect upon the results, rather than to take real action". A team could maybe run a "practice meeting" to test out a new meeting protocol. But most of a team's activities cannot be turned into practice sessions: you cannot really launch a new product or engage with a key client "just for practice" and claim that the performance or result doesn't count. The impact of the product launch or the client session has concrete repercussions for the team and the organization.

Teams in organizations need to embed practice and reflection into their regular work routines. They should consider each interaction or session as a routine that can be analyzed as if it were a practice run to become a better team, even if—different from the idea of practice—the result of those interactions did in fact count. Too often the team norms, rules of conduct, and task or process goals are referred to a couple of times per year or only dusted off when an issue arises. They should be part of every team interaction. At each team activity, one team member can take on the role of "team guardian" and ask their peers at the beginning or end of the meeting, "What did we do today that supported our team norms?" or "How did Bob fulfill the gatekeeper role in this meeting?" Check-ins can also be more general, allowing for more open reflection and exchange: "What did we do well? What could we do better?" "What should we stop, start, or continue to do?" or "How does each team member rate the team on … (specific goal, process, rule)?" This is not the task of the team leader;

"team guardian" is an agreed-upon role that can be rotated amongst team members. According to Anthony et al., DBS introduced into their meetings the role of "joyful observer" who at the end of the meeting gives feedback to the meeting organizer in front of all participants about what went well and what could be improved in a next meeting.

Practice and learning should be part of the actual daily work. It should not be events that are organized on an off-site location with a third party expert providing the guidance. Make check-ins part of the regular work, even when everything goes well and there seems to be not much to improve. These allow small issues to be raised before they become a problem or lead to a major failure. When team members get used to and know that these check-ins are coming, they will hold themselves accountable, and this creates the sense of continuous improvement both in the team's performance and the team processes. What Manfred Kets de Vries and Konstantin Korotov describe as essential to leadership development is equally essential to the development of a team:

> Leadership development is about action and reflection and both are necessary in order to develop critical skills such as analysis, strategic planning, and critical consciousness. Without space for reflection one's ability to lead will not evolve.

Psychological safety does not emerge after a team-building day or the annual retreat. It doesn't just happen with a handful of team meetings. It takes effort, and time, to build it up. And just like developing an athletic skill, the work is never "done". As a leader, your main contribution is to create the framework and atmosphere, lead by example, build up the appropriate team routines and practices, and then step back to allow the team connections to develop and strengthen. The rewards are very significant: a team that learns, grows, and takes responsibility, even when you are not there.

CONCLUSION

When building sustainability, be aware that a team is the natural environment for humans to feel motivated and engaged, and to thrive! Working with others and being valued as a member of the team is in fact hardwired in our brains.

When members of a team feel safe enough to take interpersonal risks and be upfront when they make mistakes or have a doubt, the team is creating an environment in which members can learn and perform together. Team psychological safety is the glue that holds a team together over time, allowing it to be creative, solve problems, learn, and reach higher performance, not just for a few quarters, but in a positive and sustainable way. To develop a sustainable team, you should:

- Build up the habit of mutual support, and start when there is no urgent need using the Needs and Offers technique
- Make asking for help a way to connect and learn using the "HELP!" Board technique
- Practice dealing positively with tensions and conflicts, and ensure the team's time is spent on the strategic priorities using the Team To-Do List technique
- Talk about small and trivial mistakes and learn from them using the 50 Shades of Mistakes technique
- Consider each team interaction or session as a practice round and reflect on what went well and what to change for next time

UNLEASHING THE LIMITLESS POSSIBILITIES OF

Teams

In Part One I invited you to think—for real—about teams, and hopefully, by the end of that part you were convinced or at least intrigued by the idea of developing high-performance teams. In Part Two we went practical and started off with the basics needed to build a team, and then moved to more advanced team frameworks and creating team psychological safety to set the team up for sustained growth.

So you might ask: Is that it? Is that all there is about teams? In Part Three, I invite you to think—or rather, to imagine—once again. I could describe more tools, models, or techniques, but I won't do that. If you use the tools described in Part Two, you will make a significant impact in the teams you work with or are part of. Rather than add more tools, I suggest that you explore the possibilities and fill in what your teams need by yourself.

This part looks at how you can use teams to build the seemingly ever-elusive engagement so many organizations are looking for, and how teams really are the foundation from which to create your organization's future. The concept of a team's social capital illustrates that a team really has no limits if team members can explore social capital as a source of continued development and growth.

The final chapter in Part Three invites you to think, again, about yourself. More particularly, about what kind of leader you want to be remembered as. Only you can make the choice whether to use teams as the foundation of your legacy or not.

In Part Three we also meet Susan. Susan joins Widget International as a managing director, just like James. In her first 18 months, Susan is faced with the same challenges as James but she deals with them quite differently. Like James, Susan is an imaginary character. She is not super-woman and has not climbed Mount Everest. She looks at the challenges she encounters and reacts to them with a deliberate focus on building a team. After 18 months and lots of energy spent, Susan still has plenty of things to do, but she finds herself in a different state of mind than James.

A TALE OF TWO TEAMS: SUSAN

Susan finally had a long weekend to herself and decided to spend some time in a hotel on the beach. It had been a busy 18 months since she joined Widgets International as its managing director. Although lots remained to do, she felt satisfied with the progress so far, especially with her leadership team.

It had been a great start when she was hired by the CEO to lead the organization. Although her experience was in a very different industry, her focus on building a high-performance leadership team seemed to have impressed the CEO. After a lackluster three years under the previous managing director, it seemed the CEO was ready for a new approach, as long as performance was in line with expectations.

The first two months, Susan spent time getting to know all the key people in the headquarters and travelled to the key subsidiaries to get a good sense of what Widgets International was about and of the challenges ahead. She did not make any decisions but listened and learned. She got to know her leadership team well with several one-on-one discussions and a dinner with each of them, as well as a few lunches with the whole team. Susan also answered any questions her leadership had about her and her experience.

During her discussions, she quickly found out that the quality manager felt bored in the role he had been filling for three years, and that he seemed interested in the vacancy in the logistics role. Susan asked him plenty of questions and talked to the human resources manager and a few key members in the logistics team about the possible role change, and was impressed with the quality manager's motivation to make a significant career change and his eagerness to learn. The quality manager also proposed one of his own direct reports to succeed him. Although junior and lacking the managerial experience, this young engineer seemed ready for a step up. Susan obtained input from all the important players and decided to go ahead with the change. She asked the human resources manager to inform the leadership team and create a transition and communication program.

In her exchanges, she found out the leadership team spent two hours each week sitting in the large conference room going through tons of PowerPoint slides, and that each of them spent about as much time to prepare these slides. When she asked about the outcome of these meetings, it seemed there was very little to show for them. It was just how things had been done for several years. She changed the meeting format and reviewed each manager's key indicators in the one-on-one sessions she had with them, and sometimes asked some members of the manager's team to join in. The leadership meeting was changed to a bimonthly meeting with a new format. No more PowerPoint. Each manager came prepared to share three things that went well in their department, three challenges they were facing, and three areas where they needed help. After a bit of a difficult start, the team got the hang of the meeting and very soon, Susan saw them exchange amongst themselves rather than just report their issues to her. The requests for help were mostly answered during the meeting. In addition, Susan always had one item for discussion, brainstorming, and gathering ideas. After a few months, Susan added one topic to the meeting agenda: each team member would share a mistake they had made in the previous two weeks and what they had learned from the mistake. The team voted at each bimonthly meeting for the "most praiseworthy" mistake and the manager who had shared that mistake was awarded the "learning hero" badge for the following two weeks. The different key indicators were summarized on a large board in the lunch area, so the status of the business was visible to all.

Susan enjoyed the exchanges with the different members of the leadership team and decided to adjust the one-on-one meetings with each of them. From reporting updates, these discussions turned into coaching sessions where Susan could explore with each manager the issues they were facing and look at how she could support them. In some discussions, managers indicated that some of their peers were not helping as much as they could. Rather than trying to patch up these gaps by herself, Susan explored how the team members could solve whatever issue they had directly. She also made sure to follow up during the next meeting to find out how things had changed. Little by little, she also used these sessions to ask for feedback about her own leadership style. Not much happened the first couple of times. She then started to be more pragmatic and asked each team member to list three things she as managing director would either need to start or stop doing. She acted on more than 70% of the suggestions and this started to create a climate of trust where the leadership team saw that Susan was sincere about improving and developing herself.

Susan didn't believe that 15 people could efficiently work together, so she set up sub-teams for specific priorities. At any time, the leadership team was running four or five parallel teams focusing on separate issues. Susan was part of about half of these teams. The teams shared a short update on their projects or initiatives in the bimonthly team meetings. In the first six months, one team looked at improving the results of the engagement survey that had been administered the year before, focusing on the areas where improvement was needed. Another team developed a plan for up-selling more advanced widgets to the main existing customers. A third one launched an initiative with external support to streamline inter-department reporting steps and cut out any non-value-added work.

About six months into the new role, Susan was quite comfortable with the team dynamic, the mix of one-on-one sessions and team meetings, and the atmosphere overall. She felt she had a good grasp on each team member's strengths and weaknesses. She was now ready to prepare the plan for Widgets International's next three years. She prepared this critical work with an external facilitator who proposed a two-day retreat for building a three-year plan with detailed priorities for the first year. Susan spent many hours making sure the facilitator understood the purpose of the retreat well, and also that this would be a real collaborative effort so that each member of the leadership team would adhere to and commit to the strategic and operational plan. The two days went very well, and although Susan had known each of the team members quite well by then, she was positively impressed by how some of them contributed to and enhanced the work done by the team. Yet she was also a bit disappointed by a few others and she later discussed her observations with them in their one-on-one meetings. What was most to her liking was that the plan that was built over the two days was really the team's plan for Widgets International, not just Susan's plan. Susan invited the CEO to join them during the last two hours of the second day, and sat next to him while her team presented the main axes of the plan. The team's enthusiasm and motivation were clear for all to see. The CEO's input allowed them to fine-tune a few important parts of the plan.

After about one year in the role, Susan asked the human resources manager to organize a team-building weekend away from the office. She described to the human resources manager that she wanted a team-building retreat with meaning, focusing on conversations, and with the purpose of getting to know one another better. The human resources manager worked with the operations manager on the retreat, and those two days resulted in one of the best team events of the entire year. The team developed a team canvas with a description of the team purpose, the strengths of each of the members, the norms it committed to, and the top five team tasks for the coming six months. At each subsequent team meeting, project meeting, or activity update, ten minutes were used at the end to reflect on how the meeting had adhered to the team canvas and what gaps remained.

When the operations manager left, Susan was a bit disappointed but not surprised. This had been a topic of their discussions for a few months. Susan tried to encourage him to stay but, in the end, he preferred to move to a different city closer to where his partner lived. The relationship Susan had built up with him allowed the team to smartly prepare for the change. A new manager joined the team but until that new team member joined, the engineering manager and quality manager took over several key tasks that they had become familiar with while working with the operations manager. That gave Susan the time to focus on the recruitment. Instead of just interviewing by herself, she invited several managers from her leadership team to participate in discussions with the shortlisted candidates.

It was crazy how fast 18 months had flown by. Susan was overall happy with how things were going. Not all the indicators were where they should be, but the team dynamic and mutual support clearly signaled to Susan that those gaps would be filled. The team had met most of the targets of the one-year operational plan and were getting ready to fine-tune next year's priorities. Susan set her own priority of rotating her leadership role amongst some of her direct reports. Even if she had committed to the CEO to staying three years in the role, she wanted to create a shortlist of those who could follow in her footsteps. And the best way was to put them in the actual leadership role and see how each of them coped. Susan was excited to start the second half of her tenure at Widgets International.

PUSHING THE BOUNDARIES

What if there really is no limit
to your team's potential?

The earlier sections gave you several insights and actions or techniques—and hopefully solid motivation—to move from the basics to more advanced team routines. In this last section, there are no more tips or techniques to add to the list. Rather, there are several reflections that hopefully will inspire you even more to see the enormous untapped potential that teams hold.

ENGAGEMENT THROUGH TEAMS

The Gallup organization has been measuring engagement for decades. Their surveys broadly identified three categories of employees with respect to engagement at work. First, there are the highly engaged employees, those who live and breathe for the organization, go above and beyond what is expected of them, and talk positively about their organization to whomever they meet. These are your fully engaged dream employees. Then there is the middle group, those who show up, do their jobs (most of the time), and clock out at the end of their roster. They do what is required of them but see the organization as just the entity that gives them their paychecks in exchange for their contributions. They are not engaged. Then there is the third group of the actively disengaged. Although they come to work and do their jobs, they do the absolute minimum (at best), try and hurt the company when they can, badmouth it to anyone who wants to listen, and look to create tensions around them. This third group of disengaged employees is a scary one. But fortunately, Gallup surveys around the world indicate that on average only about 15% of employees fall into this category. The highly engaged group represents about 30% of the surveyed employees, and the rest or about 55% fall into the not engaged group.

Organizations spend lots of resources trying to move those in the not engaged category to the highly engaged category (and minimize the impact of the disengaged). These efforts are either at the level of the organization or the individual. At the level of the organization, there will be programs to "change the culture" or to develop and communicate the vision, purpose, mission, or values. The expectation is that these ideals will inspire employees and strengthen the engagement with the organization. At the level of the individual, the focus is to identify those less engaged employees, and try to engage them directly through coaching or career opportunity discussions. In the many years and the thousands of companies Gallup has been evaluating, the levels of overall engagement have hardly changed. Despite all the efforts, training, working groups, or action plans, the percentage of people in each engagement category does not change that much, across industries and countries.

Marcus Buckingham and Ashley Goodall's research recently discovered that it is not at the level of the organization, nor at the level of the individual, but rather at the level of the team that engagement exists or evaporates: "The most effective way to build engagement is to focus not on culture or on individuals as though they work in isolation, but rather on what makes an individual's performance shine: their team." If you are looking for real impact and engagement, don't try to change culture. Build teams.

Maybe teams are the secret to developing real and lasting engagement in your organization?

TEAMS TO DEAL WITH THE VUCA WORLD

The US military coined the term VUCA (volatile, uncertain, complex, and ambiguous) to describe the realities on the battlefield when dealing with terrorist adversaries. In the pre-VUCA world, the enemy was another country or alliance of countries, with their political structures, military infrastructures, and resources. Armies had developed and trained to fight and win against this kind of enemies. The terrorist enemy did not fit that category: there was no clear command structure, infrastructure was minimal and changed all the time, and the distinction between enemy combatants and civil population became blurry. The usual military tactics or even strategies didn't work with this kind of enemy. "We were actually struggling to cope with an environment that was fundamentally different from anything we had planned or trained for," writes retired US army general Stanley McChrystal in his book.

To adapt, the US military changed its top-down command structure into what McChrystal et al. calls a "team of teams" model where leadership provided direction and purpose, but decisions and execution were left to the teams on the ground who were nearest to the most up-to-date information:

> In the old model, subordinates provided information and leaders disseminated commands. We reversed it: we had out leaders provide information so that subordinates, armed with context, understanding, and connectivity, could take the initiative and make decisions.

The business world adopted the VUCA concept to describe its competitive environment, with accelerating change, business model interruption, and rapidly evolving user needs. Business leaders have become more and more aware that the model of the heroic leader who is the central decision point of the organization is no longer viable. Experience and expertise are of limited value when the environment and challenges are so fundamentally different from how they looked just a few years ago, and very few would dare to predict the business situation in just a few months. Despite this awareness, leaders are struggling when it comes to adjusting their organizational structure to meet the needs of this uncertain environment on the one hand, and of their multi-generational employees on the other. As Ruth Wageman et al. write:

> Leadership teams are not only a feasible means of providing organizational leadership, but they are also increasingly necessary as the demands of top roles outdistance the capacities of any single person.

This evolution needs to affect the entire organization, not only the top layer. Just like the US military built a team of teams, the core of a forward-looking organization should be built around networks of teams where all members share the same values and culture, where information and feedback can flow freely, and where individuals and teams are rewarded for their skills and abilities (not their position).

Maybe a network of teams is how you and your organization can thrive in the volatile, uncertain, complex, and ambiguous world?

BUILDING YOUR ORGANIZATION'S FUTURE

Your organization will evolve, and you need to build it so it continues to grow. What do you do when you need a new leader for your marketing or engineering division? Do you recruit from the outside because none of the engineers or marketing people is ready for this responsibility? Or do you pick the best of the engineers or marketeers to be the new leader? The whole idea of developing high-potentials is so they can be your future leaders. Obviously, you need to make sure your future leaders have the required individual skills and that they can deliver performance. Yet, as explained by Wageman et al., those that get promoted in the organization often struggle to shift successfully from individual contributor to team leader:

> Most leaders are selected based on their successes as individual contributors, even if that background has often been shown to actually harm the growth of the team if the person stepping into the new role doesn't know how to make the vital shift from performer to facilitator.

Too often promotion and assessment methods focus on the individual's performance. The best way to assess how someone will perform as a team leader is to see how they work when they are part of a team. Do they overpower the others with their ideas? Or do they listen to all options and based on these propose a smart way forward? You cannot evaluate how your high-potentials work with others if the only interactions within your team are the reporting meetings. Having your high-potentials work in a team setting on a specific challenge can be very revealing. Approaches like action learning allow high-potentials to develop a role as team member, and solve real important challenges at the same time, writes Michael Marquardt et al. in their book *Optimizing the Power of Action Learning*. The process brings together a diverse group of people and asks them to find solutions for a complex organization-wide problem. Every member of the group is deemed accountable for developing strategies and solving the problem. Leadership becomes distributed and shared within the group, as Michael Marquardt, Choon Seng Ng, and Helen Goodson share in their article on team development. The experience pushes participants out of their comfort zones. How they deal with this situation will demonstrate their capabilities—or limitations—to learn and navigate in the VUCA world when they become leaders in the future. The action learning session can lead to surprises. Some who were thought of as high-potentials will confirm or even exceed their potential. Others who were under the radar jump out and positively impress the leadership team. And a few who were considered top guns actually fall flat. In one such experience, a country manager of an outsourcing firm said at the end of the series of sessions he attended: "We now know where people really stand… and in some cases that is not where we thought they were standing!"

> 66 Leaders can and should be team players,
> knowing when to guide others and when to step back,
> listen and collaborate. 99
> – Daniel Goleman, psychologist and science journalist

It is tempting (and somewhat easier) to identify high-potentials and future leaders by looking at each of them individually. But it is by having them work in a team that you really see how they stack up!

Maybe teams are where your successor is currently thriving?

YOUR TEAM'S SOCIAL CAPITAL

The concept of social capital gained popularity in the 2000s and has mostly been applied to communities. Individuals have a lot of social resources in which to dig in order to achieve a certain goal or productivity level. If I am confused about a document my bank sends me, I would most likely ask my sister who works in a bank for her advice. If someone in my own circle of friends mentions a challenge with their bank, I might think of connecting them with my sister, even if they don't know each other. I use my own social capital network to get issues resolved and may offer access to my social capital to others.

Social capital can also be interpreted at the level of a team. In a team, each member brings their professional competencies and experiences. The marketing manager has made marketing her field of expertise through years of experience. She continues to stay abreast of the latest developments in marketing, has in her network many connections in the marketing field, and knows many marketing professionals. She regularly contacts these connections in her social capital to discuss new trends in marketing or get ideas about how to deal with particular challenges. The connections in her network will similarly tap into her experience and knowledge to get ahead and deal with their marketing-related challenges. This set of experiences, connections, and contacts is what allows the marketing manager to fulfill her marketing role in the team and in the organization, and that is what her teammates and the organization as a whole expect from the individual filling the role of marketing manager.

However, the marketing manager's social capital stretches way beyond the field of marketing. She has in her network family and friends, and business and personal connections with a much wider experience than just marketing. One of her family members works for an engineering design firm. Through her children's school connections, she knows a school director who is working closely with the local authorities. Her best friend from college is now a well-known lawyer. All these connections are part of the marketing manager's social capital. She probably doesn't talk much with these contacts about her marketing role, and the school director or the lawyer most likely doesn't come to mind when she is thinking about how to deal with a specific marketing challenge.

The marketing manager's social capital can be available for her team to tap into if certain conditions are met. Maybe the marketing manager's colleague in the finance department has a legal challenge with a particular vendor. In his own network, the finance manager doesn't really know a lawyer with whom to discuss the issue. If only he knew that the marketing manager had this close connection with a lawyer, he could check if this connection could help him out. A large part of the marketing manager's social capital remains unknown and therefore unexplored and non-accessible to her team members or her organization. What are the possibilities if the marketing manager's wide range of social connections could become a source of intelligence for the team? Lieberman posits that the key to enhancing one's productivity lies in the group:

> The assumption that productivity is about smart people working hard on their own has been masking the fact that individual intelligence may only be optimized when it is enhanced through social

connections to others in the group. Social connections are essentially the original Internet connecting different pockets of intelligence to make each pocket more than it would otherwise be by itself.

As researchers Martin van der Gaag and Tom Snijders point out, social capital in a team is a function of the quality of the relationship (in other words, the quality of the connection) and the opportunity to meet; these will determine the extent to which the finance manager has access to the marketing manager's social capital (and vice versa). If the quality of the connection between the members of the team is average or below average, it is unlikely that the marketing manager would think of introducing her finance colleague to her lawyer friend from college. Even if this connection is fine, it requires more than just "getting along" for two colleagues to open up their social capital network to each other because doing so carries a risk: if the introduction doesn't work out and creates a problem, the marketing manager can be impacted in both her relationships with her lawyer friend and with her finance manager team colleague. It requires a genuine trust that this introduction will be handled appropriately, and also requires reciprocity where both members of the team are helping each other. If both the marketing manager and the finance manager support one another in this way, there will be a compounding effect on the quality of their relationship. Yet the opposite is also true: if providing access to one's social capital to a team colleague goes awry, the relationship between the team members can be irreparably damaged.

The second requirement is the opportunity to meet. If the finance and marketing manager each focus on their own areas of responsibility and if their encounters are only in the context of quarterly presentation-heavy business updates, they will not really know what is going on in the other's area, and what unresolved needs the other may have. If they meet regularly to work together, for example as members on a project team, the probability that they will become aware of the challenges and issues the other is facing and need help with is higher.

In addition to these working sessions, specific interventions help to explore—intentionally—the social capital that the whole team can tap into. The HELP! Board shared earlier in the Team Technique #2 highlight can be adapted or enhanced to invite all team members to also think of people in their network (social capital) who could help with a particular need. When team members have developed the habit of sharing, asking for help, exploring other ideas, and actively supporting each other, the team's social capital can be explored to the fullest.

If the marketing manager and finance manager become aware of the kind of connections and experiences each have in addition to their respective functional roles in marketing and finance, they would each have doubled the potential social capital they could tap into. At the level of the team, the team suddenly looks much better connected, and has the potential to be more creative and successful in dealing with the business challenges in its environment. If a team can tap into its entire social capital, it will be building a real competitive advantage that goes well beyond the simple sum of the individuals in the team.

The social capital model is a great illustration of how a team can really develop way beyond its current performance, with some minimum effort on developing the quality of its connections and the opportunities to meet.

What if there really was no limit to your team's potential?

CONCLUSION

Part Two focused on the different tactics needed to build, develop, and grow a team into a high-performance team. But there is no real limit to what a high-performance team can do. Get inspired by continuing the effort and by crafting your own journey of developing teams by keeping in mind that:

- Teams are a great ground on which to build engagement with the organization
- Teams and a network of teams can be your lever to navigate the VUCA world successfully
- Your successor should be a great team player
- A well-oiled team can leverage each team member's social capital to really extend the possibilities for growth and success

TEAMS AS YOUR LEGACY

How (or rather, by whom) do you
want to be remembered?

Civil rights activist Maya Angelou said, "At the end of the
day people won't remember what you said or did, they will
remember how you made them feel." Most likely, people
will not remember the new product you launched, the
successful cost-cutting project you led, or your excellent
sales results. The people who worked with you and around
you will remember you for how you made them feel and
for the impact you had on them. The members of the teams
you develop successfully into high-performance teams will
look up to you for the rest of their careers, whether they
work in the same company, join a different one, or start
their own.

In preparation for this book, a manager shared the
story of who in her eyes was the best team leader she had

ever worked with. She described how this leader really built connections between team members, empowered members to collaborate and learn from each other, and overall delivered results while maintaining a positive team dynamic. When that team leader moved on to another responsibility within the same company, his successor didn't pay much attention to developing the team. The team dynamic rather quickly disappeared, the team became a set of managers reporting to the new team leader, and once in a while, sharing updates to others in the team in the monthly meeting. The successor had made the choice (conscious or not) not to focus on maintaining or developing the team. This must have been quite a disappointment for the first team leader who now saw his efforts disintegrating. But should that be a reason not to continue building teams? I don't think so, and neither did the first team leader. He moved on and continued to apply his approach to leading and building teams. He never received the "best team leader" award in his organization (that award did not exist) but he positively impacted all those he worked with in the different roles he had. Most of us cannot change the world. But over the lifespan of a career you can probably impact several dozens of people with whom you work. How would it make you feel if someone names you as their most inspiring and motivating team leader? Maybe teams should be what your legacy is really about?

Your leadership journey may depend on many external factors and circumstances. But the choice to build your leadership and your legacy by building, developing, and growing your teams, is yours.

AFTERWORD

Whatever you have been doing up to now when it comes to thinking about and acting on teams, I hope this book has given you some new energy, new inspiration, and conviction that, although there is no magic formula, you are very much capable of making a big impact on your team, whether you are leading it or a part of it. It is your choice what you want to do from here forward.

Do you go back to how James dealt with the different challenges he encountered when given the chance to lead a team? For sure there will be situations where you will be tempted to take James' shortcuts that seem to make sense in the short term. Or maybe you are inspired to try and build a team like Susan did?

If you are not really convinced that you want to make teams a central part of your leadership, I think there is no point in "trying" some of the tools and techniques proposed in this book. If you are convinced, then I hope you will start to look for opportunities to implement the ideas and suggestions listed in Parts Two and Three. Once you are on your way, making sure the basics are in place and remain in place, you will be more confident to look for other approaches that can support you and your team. Your team is both a reflection of yourself and your limits. At the same time, you can shine through your team and explore the endless possibilities a healthy team brings, with benefits for everyone in and around the team. Here's to you and your leadership legacy through teams!

BIBLIOGRAPHY

Andreatta, Britt. "Better Together: The Neuroscience of Teams." *Association for Talent Development*, May 4, 2017, www.td.org/insights/better-together-the-neuroscience-of-teams

Andreatta, Britt. *Wired to Connect: The Brain Science of Teams and a New Model for Creating Collaboration and Inclusion.* 7th Mind Publishing, 2018.

Anthony, Scott D., et al. "Breaking Down the Barriers to Innovation: Build the Habits and Routines That Lead to Growth." *Harvard Business Review*, 2019.

Banks, Shannon. *Social Leadership.* Amsterdam: World Institute for Action Learning.

Beebe, Steven A., and John T. Masterson. *Communicating in Small Groups: Principles and Practices.* 11th ed: Pearson, 2016.

Buckingham, Marcus, and Ashley Goodall. "The Power of Hidden Teams." *Harvard Business Review*, 2019.

Byford, M., M. Watkins, and L. Triantogiannis. "Onboarding Isn't Enough." *Harvard Business Review*, 2017.

Carlson, Nicholas. *Marissa Mayer and the Fight to Save Yahoo!* New York: Twelve, 2015.

Collins, Jim. "First Who, Then What." *Jim Collins*, www. jimcollins.com/concepts/first-who-then-what.html

Collins, Jim. *Good to Great: Why Some Companies Make the Leap ... And Others Don't.* New York, NY: HarperBusiness, 2001.

Coyle, Daniel. *The Culture Code: The Secrets of Highly Successful Groups.* Bantam, 2018.

Csikszentmihalyi, Mihaly. *Flow; the Psychology of Optimal Experience.* Harper Perennial, 1990.

Duhigg, Charles. "What Google Learned from Its Quest to Build the Perfect Team." *New York Times* 2016.

Edmondson, Amy C. *The Fearless Organization: Creating Psychological Safety in the Workplace for Learning, Innovation, and Growth.* Wiley, 2018.

Edmondson, Amy C. "Psychological Safety and Learning Behavior in Work Teams." *Administrative Science Quarterly* 44.2 (1999): 350-83.

Edmondson, Amy C. "Psychological Safety, Trust, and Learning: A Group-Level Lens." *Trust and Distrust in Organizations: Dilemmas and Approaches.* Eds. Kramer, R. and K. Cook. New York: Russel Sage Foundation, 2004. 239-72.

Edmondson, Amy C. *Teaming: How Organizations Learn, Innovate, and Compete in the Knowledge Economy.* San Francisco, CA: Jossey-Bass, 2012.

Florian Kratz, Ellen. "Get Me a CEO from GE!" *Fortune,* 2005. "Gallup Q12 Survey." *Gallup.* q12.gallup.com

Grant, Adam. *Give and Take: Why Helping Others Drives Our Success.* Penguin Books, 2014.

Grant, Heidi. "How to Get the Help You Need." *Harvard Business Review*, 2018.

Heffernan, Margaret. "Forget the Pecking Order at Work." TED, June 16, 2015, www.ted.com/talks/ margaret_heffernan_forget_the_pecking_order_at_ work?language=en.

Johnson, David, and Roger Johnson. *Cooperation and Competition: Theory and Research.* Edina: Interaction Book Company, 1989.

Kegan, Robert, and Lisa Laskow Lahey. *An Everyone Culture, Becoming a Deliberately Developmental Organization.* Harvard Business Review Press, 2016.

Keller, Scott, and Mary Meaney. *Leading Organizations: Ten Timeless Truths.* Bloomsbury Business, 2017.

Kets de Vries, Manfred, and Konstantin Korotov. "Developing Leaders and Leadership Development." INSEAD, 2010.

Lencioni, Patrick. *Overcoming the Five Dysfunctions of a Team: A Field Guide for Leaders, Managers, and Facilitators.* Jossey-Bass, 2005.

Lieberman, Matthew D. *Social: Why Our Brains Are Wired to Connect.* Broadway Books, 2014.

Locke, Edwin A., and Gary P. Latham. *A Theory of Goal Setting & Task Performance.* Prentice Hall, 1990.

Marquardt, Michael, et al. *Optimizing the Power of Action Learning: Real-Time Strategies for Developing Leaders, Building Teams and Transforming Organizations.* 3rd ed: Nicholas Brealey, 2018.

Marquardt, Michael, Choon Seng Ng, and Helen Goodson. "Team Development Via Action Learning." *Advances in Developing Human Resources*, 2010.

Martin, Andre, and Vidula Bal. The State of Teams. Center for Creative Leadership, 2015.

Maslow, Abraham. *Motivation and Personality*. New York: Harper and Row, 1954.

McChrystal, Stanley, et al. *Team of Teams: New Rules of Engagement for a Complex World*. Portfolio, 2015.

"Measurable Results." *Team Coaching International*, 2020. teamcoachinginternational.com/what-is-measured/

Miyahara, Helena Mihoko. "A New Way to Select New Recruits." *WIAL Global Newsletter*, 2016.

Muir, W. M. "Genetics and the Behaviour of Chickens: Welfare and Productivity." *Genetics and the Behaviour of Domestic Animals*. Eds. Grandin, Temple and Mark Deesing. 2nd ed: Academic Press, 2013.

Nunes, Debra. "Just Not Part of the Team." *Briefings Magazine*. Korn Ferry, 2020, www.kornferry.com/insights/articles/just-not-part-of-the-team.

Postman, Neil, and Charles Weingartner. *Teaching as a Subversive Activity*. New York: Delacorte Press, 1969.

Revans, Reginald William. *ABC of Action Learning*. Gower Publishing, Ltd., 2011.

Reynolds, Alison, and David Lewis. "The Two Traits of the Best Problem-Solving Teams." *Harvard Business Review*, 2018.

Rock, David. "Scarf: A Brain-Based Model for Collaborating with and Influencing Others." *Neuroleadership Journal* 1.1 (2008).

Rozovsky, Julia. "The Five Keys to a Successful Google Team." *re:Work*, Google, November 17, 2015, rework.withgoogle. com/blog/five-keys-to-a-successful-google-team/

Schwartz, Jeff, et al. "Global Human Capital Trends 2016." Deloitte University Press, 2016, www2.deloitte. com/content/dam/Deloitte/global/Documents/ HumanCapital/gx-dup-global-human-capital-trends-2016.pdf

Schwartz, Roger. *Smart Leaders, Smarter Teams: How You and Your Team Get Unstuck to Get Results.* Jossey-Bass, 2013.

Shapiro, Mary. *HBR Guide to Leading Teams.* Harvard Business Review Press, 2015.

Sobel, Andrew, and Jeroid Panas. *Power Questions: Build Relationships, Win New Business, and Influence Others.* Wiley, 2012.

Sull, Donald, Rebecca Homkes, and Charles Sull. "Why Strategy Execution Unravels and What to Do About It." *Harvard Business Review*, 2015.

Tuckman, Bruce W. "Developmental Sequence in Small Groups." *Psychological Bulletin* 63.6 (1965): 384–99.

Vaillant, George E. *Triumphs of Experience: The Men of the Harvard Grant Study.* Belknap Press, 2015.

van der Gaag, Martin, and Tom Snijders. "An Approach to the Measurement of Individual Social Capital." *SCALE Conference on Social Capital*, 2002.

Wageman, Ruth, et al. *Senior Leadership Teams: What It Takes to Make Them Great*. Harvard Business Review Press, 2008.

Watkins, Michael. *The First 90 Days: Critical Success Strategies for New Leaders at All Levels*. Boston, Mas: Harvard Business School Press, 2003.

Watkins, Michael. "Leading the Talent You Inherit." *Harvard Business Review*, 2016.

"What Is Action Learning?" *World Institute for Action Learning*, 2020, wial.org/action-learning/

FREE BONUS

Are you fired up and ready to get serious about developing your team? Assuming you have the basics in place, you can get ready for the next step by measuring the level of psychological safety in your team. A simple anonymous survey allows you to visualize the team's overall level of psychological safety, as well as identify which of the elements that constitute team psychological safety are strengths and which need improvement in your team.

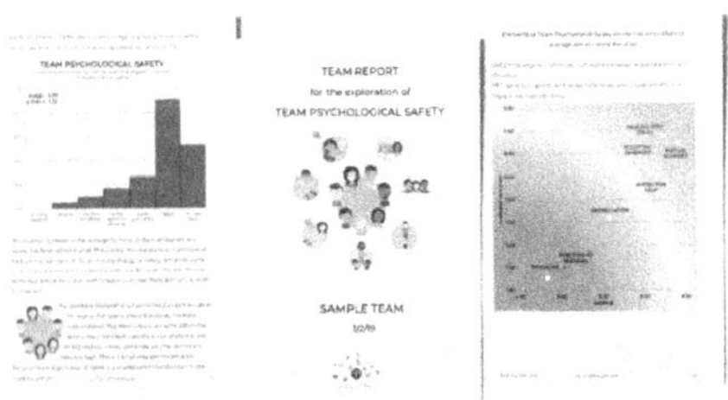

As a bonus with this book, you can get the survey and a 30-page report of its results, valued at USD300, for free! Send an email to peter@teamasone.com with an image of your book purchase receipt, and you can start the survey right away!

More details at

www.teamasone.com

ABOUT THE AUTHOR

Peter Cauwelier, PhD, is a highly qualified team coach with more than 20 years of experience in operations with multinational companies. He is the founder of ASIO Consulting (www.teamasone.com), an independent consulting business focusing on the organizational development of teams. Based on his experience and research, Peter created the Team Psychological Safety Certified Facilitator program to help coaches and consultants deliver more impact to the teams they work with. A Master Action Learning Coach, Peter is the President of the World Institute for Action Learning and the founder of WIAL Thailand. Peter has worked with teams at Bangkok Airways, Banpu, Charn Issara, Decathlon, Dextra Asia, Nestlé, Mane, Mazars, Michelin, Safran, Salesforce, Takeda, TATA Motors, Thomson Reuters, Tipco, Total, and Yum!

AGILE AND INNOVATIVE SOLUTIONS FOR PROBLEM SOLVING AND ORGANIZATIONAL DEVELOPMENT

❚❚ ACTION LEARNING ❚❚

is a problem-solving process that involves a small group working on a real business problem, taking action and learning as individuals, as a team, and as an organization.

❚❚ ACTION LEARNING ❚❚

helps your team solve problems, learn from the experience, and develop the competencies of the members and the team as a whole. All at the same time.

Are important cross-functional problems solved by the people involved, or do they always end up on your desk ?

Are members working as high-performance teams or is collaboration just a slogan on the wall ?

Are your team members really turning into leaders once they return from the expensive leadership development program?

Is your team learning from each experience and using the learning to increase performance? Or is it stuck in a day-by-day very-busy approach?

Are managers coaching their respective teams? Or is coaching outsourced?

> *"There can be no learning without action and no action without learning"*
>
> — Reg Revans —

WIAL Thailand offers :

✓ Certification programs to equip your managers to lead their team as an Action Learning coach
✓ Customized team development programs and coaching services by a WIAL certified Master Action Learning Coach to support your team solving complex company-wide problems while learning at the same time

WIAL Thailand, the official WIAL affiliate in Thailand

✉ peter@wialthailand.com   ☎ + 66 81 939 7833   ❚ Action Learning in Thailand

Calling All Professionals, Business Owners and Entrepreneurs, Speakers and Trainers, Coaches and Consultants, Property Agents and Financial Planners

So You Want To Be An Author

Developing Your Blueprint for Publishing Success

4 REASONS WHY YOU SHOULD BE A PUBLISHED AUTHOR

- Pump up your visibility and increase your presence in the market. With the expanded mindshare you enjoy, you are able to attract more prospects and partners knocking on your door.
- Establish authority in the market without the need to brag. Because book authors are viewed as experts in their field, the trust you gain helps you to convert prospects to better, higher paying clients quickly.
- Build your personal brand and boost your credibility without having to spend thousands of dollars to run expensive advertising or marketing campaigns.
- Spread your ideas to a wider audience even without your physical presence. A book is like a name card on steroids helping you to spread your message and promote you and your business while you are sleeping.

So You Want To Be An Author is a 6-module virtual hands-on authorship masterclass specifically tailored to help game changers like you who aspire to stay at the top of their game by becoming published authors of non-fiction books. In this workshop, you will be guided to develop your own personal blueprint for publishing success using our 6P Framework of Publishing™. This the exactly the same proven framework that over 300 of our authors have followed to take them from just having an idea in their mind to enjoying success today as published authors.

Plan ▸ Pen ▸ Prepare ▸ Produce ▸ Promote ▸ Publicise

- How to identify a niche and develop the contents for a book
- How to nurture your book from idea to market
- What are the critical success factors that can make or break a book
- How to get others to pay for your book before it is even published
- What you must do to market your book to gain maximum exposure
- How to generate free publicity for you, your book and your business

REGISTER TODAY:

https://candidcreation.com/services/authorship-virtual-masterclass/

Kok Hwa's 'So You Want to be an Author' workshop created the spark that gave me the confidence that I was capable of writing and publishing my own book. The structure of the workshop is simple yet very clear and I am referring back to the handouts and my notes regularly. Although I did procrastinate longer than I would have liked, in the end I completed the book and am very happy with the journey and the result."

– Peter Cauwelier, Chief Team Connector, TEAM.AS.ONE
President, World Institute for Action Learning

Workshop facilitators

Phoon Kok Hwa is a Publisher at Candid Creation Publishing, where he has spent the last decade helping hundreds of aspiring authors to get their books written, published, distributed and marketed. Kok Hwa is a literary agent at heart, nurturing and extracting the potential book out of every aspiring author. Apart from his personal beliefs in author expression, he also believes in a pragmatic aspect to publishing a book–personal branding– often stating that nothing produces instant credibility faster than giving away a book as a calling card. Kok Hwa is also a certified as a Professional Action Learning Coach by the World Institute for Action Learning and also a recipient of the International Coaching Excellence Award 2015.

Andrew Chow is a passionate social media and public relations strategist, entrepreneur, speaker and author of *Social Media 247*, *Public Relations 247*, and *Personal Branding 247*. Based in Singapore, his insights into social media strategy, media management and entrepreneurship have made him a choice selection for workshops and public speaking engagements across Asia,through which he educates professionals on how to leverage social channels for business results. Andrew's career has seen him work with an array of clients including AXA Insurance, Abbot Medical Optics, Singtel and Sony Pictures.

ALUMNI HALL OF FAME

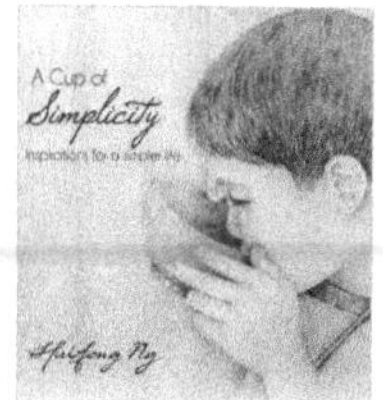

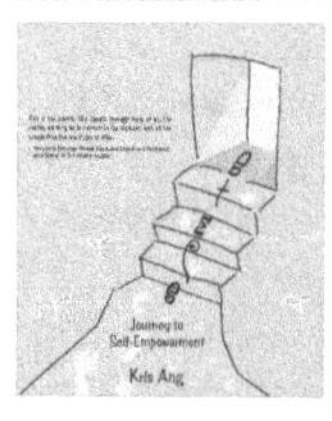

Order your copy today at http://candidcreation.com/bookshop/